WHEN SO

Things You Need To Know And Do

WHEN SOMEONE DIES

DIES

Things you need
to know and do

Estelle Catlett

RIGHT WAY

Typeset in 11/13pt Times by Letterpart Limited, Reigate, Surrey.

Printed and bound in Great Britain by Cox & Wyman Ltd., Reading, Berkshire.

The *Right Way* series is published by Elliot Right Way Books, Brighton Road, Lower Kingswood, Tadworth, Surrey, KT20 6TD, U.K. For information about our company and the other books we publish, visit our web site at www.right-way.co.uk

CONTENTS

INTRODUCTION

We all have to come to terms with death at some time, but, when a loved member of the family or a close friend dies, there may be no one except you to deal with all the formalities surrounding the death and to make all the necessary arrangements. There is no time immediately to mourn the passing; things have to be done. If you have never had to deal with a death before and you have no knowledge of what to do, it can be very daunting.

Particularly difficult are cases of elderly couples where one spouse dies. In many instances, the husband, feeling that he is protecting his wife, has always assumed responsibility for all their financial affairs. On his death, the surviving widow is left to deal with all the necessary funeral and financial matters but has no knowledge of her financial situation, does not even know the name of the bank her husband used and has, in fact, never even had to write a cheque. The reverse may apply when the husband, who has no knowledge of running the household and paying the household bills, is left.

Another difficult situation is when one partner, in a young couple with children, dies. The surviving partner not only has to deal with all the financial and funeral arrangements but also to cope with a family of small children.

We have to learn to deal with the formalities and legal requirements of death very quickly and I hope that this book will help you. It is not a book about the emotional side of bereavement because we all have different ways of coping (although inevitably some reference will be made to dealing with bereavement and the names and addresses of bereavement counsellors and organisations specifically dealing with this field are given in Appendix II). This book is a practical guide through the bureaucratic maze, based on personal experience and that of some of my friends. Practices, Probate and laws may differ in Scotland and Northern Ireland, but I hope that the general advice is helpful.

In whatever way we deal with the traumatic events that occur in our lives, one thing is necessary for all of us: that is to keep a sense of humour. Funny things do happen at funerals and when making arrangements after the death. Do not be afraid to laugh if something amusing happens. It is not disrespectful to see the funny side of things. If the deceased had a good sense of humour, he or she would have appreciated funny situations *whenever* they occurred. Happy memories of the deceased person will sustain you through this difficult time.

Seeking Help

You may find that you need help for many reasons. Help could come from unexpected sources: neighbours you have not previously known, tradesmen and Social Services. Even if you are normally reluctant to seek help, accept offers of assistance, provided they are really helpful and not just intrusive.

Most people you will have to deal with will be helpful, but it should be remembered that you are only one of many needing their advice and assistance and they will not necessarily be able to give you all the time you feel you need. You may well be asked questions about the deceased and yourself which you feel are intrusive, irrelevant and downright silly, but people in certain positions have an agenda to follow and will continue to apply the rules whether they are appropriate in your case or not. Having told someone that I was the sole surviving relative of my aunt, I was then asked 'Is her husband alive?'! He then continued relentlessly to ask every prepared question on his form, most of which were quite pointless.

Before visiting or speaking on the telephone to the various government and local departments, or anyone else in an official capacity regarding the deceased, make a written note of all the questions you wish to ask. That way you will not forget an important point you need to raise. You can also jot down any answers you receive.

When completing the numerous forms and questionnaires that are required, if you have to send them away try to keep a photocopy of each document or letter that you write. This will assist you if there are any queries arising from the information that you have written on the forms. There are many shops these days where you can make photocopies of documents. Very often a Post Office or newsagent will have a photocopy machine. There are also specialist copy shops.

Funeral directors are usually very helpful and kindly people. They are used to dealing with these matters on a day-to-day basis. It is their work, but they are not insensitive to their clients' needs. You will be paying for their services so take advantage of their help and knowledge. Ask as many questions and take as much time as you wish.

1

AT THE DEATH

Death in a Hospital or Hospice
It may be that this is your first close experience with death. If the dying person is in a hospital or a hospice and you wish to be with him, most such institutions are very accommodating and will allow you to remain at the bedside. If you are alone, someone from the hospital or hospice will probably keep an eye on you.

If you know that the person would find comfort from a minister or priest, particularly if he is a member of the Roman Catholic Church, request the priest's presence. Most hospitals and hospices have a chaplain who is in contact with local religious bodies and can arrange this. If you know which church, chapel or synagogue the person attended, ask the hospital chaplain to get in touch with it.

The doctors will have a fairly good idea of how long the person is likely to live and, if asked, will be as frank as they can be. Although someone may have suffered from a serious life-threatening illness, the specific cause of death is often pneumonia. Usually the actual death is a quiet and peaceful passing away, particularly if the person has been ill and is sedated. You may not even be aware of the moment of death. You can call for the doctor or nurse if you think that death has occurred. You will be asked to leave the room to allow the doctor to make the necessary tests to verify that death has taken place. Then you will normally be allowed to stay with the deceased to say your goodbyes undisturbed for as long as you wish.

After the Death – Death in Hospital

If the death is from natural causes and occurred in a hospital, the body will be placed in the mortuary after the doctor has certified the time, date and cause of death. The hospital will ask you to attend at their office, probably the following day, to receive the deceased's personal belongings, such as any jewellery, money, keys and clothes that he had with him in the hospital. The hospital office will give you a doctor's certificate of death which will enable you to register the death at the local office of the Registrar of Births, Deaths and Marriages.

Hospital Post Mortem

In some cases the hospital may wish to carry out a post mortem examination to find out more about the illness or cause of death suffered by the deceased. This does not involve the coroner and the hospital cannot undertake such a post mortem without the consent of the next of kin.

Organ Donation

If it is felt that a patient in hospital, under the age of 75 years, is a suitable person to be an organ donor for transplant and he is considered by the doctors to be 'brain dead' the doctor may make a request for the donation of organs, such as heart, lungs, kidneys and eye corneas. This might occur when the patient has been involved in an accident causing a head injury, or for any other reason where the brain has been deprived of oxygen, leaving the major organs available for donation. If you know that the patient carried a donor card giving consent to using organs for transplant, you will have no problem in agreeing to the doctor's request. Otherwise consent must be obtained from the next of kin, a surviving relative or the person responsible for the deceased.

Medical Research

If the deceased has left instructions that his body should be donated for medical research, the executor or next of kin should advise H M Inspector of Anatomy (see Appendix II) as soon as possible after the death. The deceased should have completed the necessary forms for this to take place and left them with a member of the family or a solicitor. If the death took place in a hospital, the hospital manager may be able to advise and assist with this.

It must be realised that even if a body is offered for medical research, for various reasons it will not always be accepted and preliminary preparations should be made for a funeral. If the body is accepted, arrangements will be made for it to be taken to the medical school. The death should be registered in the normal way. No further arrangements need to be made by the executors or next of kin. The medical school will organise and pay for a simple funeral (cremation or burial) but, if requested, the body will be returned to the family who can make their own funeral arrangements at their own expense.

Registering the Death

Once you have the doctor's certificate you will be able to register the death at the office of the Registrar of Births, Deaths and Marriages. The hospital or the home doctor will be able to tell you the address of that office. It is usually in a local Town Hall or municipal building. The Registrar may have an office in the hospital where the death can be registered. The hospital manager can advise you if it is possible to register the death at the hospital.

It is not essential to register the death on the actual date of death, but in England, Wales and Northern Ireland, unless the coroner is involved, the death must be registered within five days of the death. In Scotland death must be registered within eight days of the actual death.

Present at the Death – at Home

If the person is dying at home, it is a good idea if you have someone else there with you. You will not have the help of professional people around you as you would in a hospital or hospice. Perhaps another friend, family member of the deceased or a personal friend of your own would be suitable. If the dying person makes a request for someone particular to be present, try to arrange this. If you think that the presence of a priest or religious advisor would be of benefit, then try to arrange for him to be there. This is important for a person of the Catholic faith and you may know the name of the Parish Priest who you can contact. If a doctor has been recently attending, it would be helpful to have him present or at least be aware of the situation.

Once the death has occurred it is essential that the attending doctor be informed. It is a difficult time, but it is helpful if you can make a note of the actual time of the death as this will assist the doctor who will be required to issue the doctor's certificate. On the certificate, the doctor will certify the time, date and cause of death. The body cannot be moved until such certification is given. Once the death is certified, the body can be removed to a mortuary or funeral chapel. Arrangements can be made through a funeral director or, if you wish to use the municipal mortuary, the doctor can make the arrangements for you. There will be a charge for this service.

The doctor can issue a certificate only if he has attended the deceased within 14 days prior to the death. If this is not the case, then the doctor should inform the coroner.

Sudden Death

If you are present at a sudden or unexpected death, wherever it happens, or there are any suspicious circumstances, you should immediately inform the police. If there is no telephone on the premises you should ask a near neighbour or a passer-by to telephone the police for you. The police will take over and attend with a medical examiner and will advise you what actions will be necessary. This will depend on where and when the death takes place. Nothing should be touched even if the body is in an undignified situation. The coroner will be involved and, in all probability, the body will be removed and an autopsy or post mortem will be necessary in order to discover the cause of the death, before a certificate of death can be issued. No action can be taken by the next of kin until the manner of death has been resolved.

It is possible, if the death has taken place in a public place outside the home or hospital, as the result of an accident or a heart attack, that someone in the family will be asked to attend at the mortuary to identify the deceased before a certificate of death can be issued.

Death of a Child

Dealing with the death of a child is even more difficult than dealing with that of an adult, but hospitals and funeral directors are particularly sensitive in such cases. In the case of a stillbirth, some hospitals will make sympathetic arrangements for disposal and for a funeral to take place within the hospital chapel or at a crematorium.

Funeral directors, cemeteries and crematoria will often make no charge for arranging a simple funeral in the case of a baby or very young child and will only charge any disbursements they have to pay. If a cremation is arranged for a very young child there may be no ashes remaining.

2

IMMEDIATE ACTION

Certain things will have to be done directly after the death. The momentum of dealing with ordinary everyday things on behalf of the deceased will help to carry you through the first few days.

It will be necessary to visit the home of the deceased to deal with immediate requirements. If the deceased was taken to hospital by ambulance as an emergency and there was no one else in the home at the time, there may be windows open, lights on, a fire burning and even the television or home computer left on. These things will need attention straightaway.

Telephone
If there is no telephone at the home, a mobile telephone would prove very useful.

Dealing with Pets
If the deceased has left any pets (cats, dogs, birds, fish, hamsters etc.), they must be looked after without delay.

It is probable that if the deceased went into hospital by appointment then he made arrangements for someone to look after his pets in his absence. A neighbour or a friend who regularly looked after the pet may be looking after it or it may have been left in the care of a cattery or kennels. If the deceased regularly used professionals to look after his pets, the address of the cattery or kennels should be amongst his papers. If you cannot find the necessary information, try telephoning local or nearby catteries and kennels to enquire whether they have the pet of the deceased. The owners of the cattery or kennels should be informed of the death of the owner of the pet. They could be asked to keep the pet until such time as something more permanent can be arranged.

If there is a fish tank with tropical fish, it will need expert attention in order to keep the heating correct, and the fish need regular feeding. A local pet shop or vet might be able to give you advice.

If the death was sudden with no arrangements having been made and neither you nor one of the family nor a friend can assume responsibility for an animal, you should contact the People's Dispensary for Sick Animals (PDSA), The Royal Society for the Prevention of Cruelty to Animals (RSPCA), or a local animal sanctuary for advice. Their telephone number will be in the telephone directory (or you could ask Directory Enquiries). If necessary they will take the animal and look after it until such time as a new permanent home can be found. If you cannot make arrangements to have a pet looked after, contact the police for advice and assistance.

Cancelling Deliveries
Newspapers and bottles of milk left outside a door are sure signs that a property is unoccupied. If there is any evidence of daily deliveries such as milk or newspapers and you can find out who delivers, the deliveries should be cancelled. Try asking the neighbours as they may also have deliveries from the same shops. If you cannot find the name of the deliverers and there are neighbours, ask them to remove

the daily deliveries of newspapers and milk until you can make other arrangements.

Royal Mail
It may be necessary to advise the postal authorities. If no one is going to be present at the home of the deceased you may wish the mail to be redirected either to yourself or to whoever is dealing with the estate. There is a charge for this service and you can obtain details and an application form from the Royal Mail.

Electrical Appliances and Heating
If the deceased's property is to be left unoccupied, switch off and unplug any electrical appliances such as the TV and radio, cooker, electric fire and microwave but leave the refrigerator and freezer switched on so that any food there is preserved for the time being. In winter, leave the heating on at a low level but in summer turn off the heating and hot water system. If you know how to, turn off the water supply, especially in winter. This will prevent an endless supply of water flowing through any burst pipes.

Food and Plants
Dispose of any perishable food not in the refrigerator, such as bread, vegetables, fruit or anything that might start to smell if left for a few days. Dispose of any flowers in vases and throw away the water, but water and keep any pot plants.

Securing the Property
Criminals are not deterred by death. They often take advantage of the fact that properties will be left empty due to the death of the occupier and word soon gets around. It is essential to make sure that the home of the deceased is as secure as possible if it is to be left unoccupied. If you

yourself can stay there or arrange for someone else to stay there, so that it is not left empty, that is the best solution. If not, ask the neighbours to keep an eye open. Advise the police that the property is unoccupied, giving them your name, address and telephone number as the keyholder and make sure that all windows and doors are securely locked. If you are leaving the property empty, make sure all back doors and garden gates are locked. If there is any washing on the line in the garden, take it into the house.

If there is a security system fitted to the property, but you do not know how to activate it or know the code number, the alarm cannot be switched on. You may be able to find the printed instructions relating to the alarm system. If not, look for the name of the manufacturers on the panel and telephone them. They will request some form of evidence that you are the person who can deal with the alarm, such as your name and address and the full name of the deceased and the code number of the system. If they are satisfied, they will advise you what to do. If they will not accept instructions by telephone, ask them to call at the premises as soon as possible. When their representative calls, make sure that you see his identification before you allow him to deal with the alarm system.

Check to see whether there are any switching devices that turn on the lights at different times. These can be very helpful and should be left activated.

Securing a Vehicle
If there is a vehicle (a car, motorbike, scooter or van), make sure that it is securely locked and switch on any alarm systems. If you know how to do it, immobilise the vehicle before leaving it by removing a small part. If there is a garage, put the vehicle in it and lock the doors.

3

THE CORONER

There are eight occasions when a death must be referred to the coroner. Those are:

1. If the death occurs in suspicious circumstances.
2. If the death is sudden or unexplained.
3. If the death is obviously by suicide.
4. If the death occurs while the person is in prison or in police custody.
5. If the death takes place during an operation or before recovery from an anaesthetic after an operation.
6. If the death happens directly or indirectly as the result of an accident.
7. If the death might be due to neglect or caused by drug abuse or poison.
8. If the death occurs as the result of an abortion.

If a coroner is involved, do not worry about this. It is the duty of the coroner to work in the interests of the deceased and his family. There should be no costs for the family if a coroner's investigation is necessary.

If the death has to be reported to a coroner, it is the coroner's duty to decide on the cause of death. The coroner is able to do this without an inquest if he feels that he has sufficient medical evidence. The coroner, or an officer of his court, will take statements from the person present at the death, the person who found the body or the relatives and also consult the medical evidence. If the coroner decides that the death is from natural causes, the next of kin will be advised. A doctor's certificate will be issued and the death can be registered. A Registrar's Certificate of Death can then be obtained.

If the coroner decides that he needs a post mortem or autopsy to assist him in his investigations he can order this without the consent of the next of kin. However, if the family object to a post mortem, possibly on religious grounds, then they should inform the coroner. The coroner may still wish to proceed with a post mortem if he thinks it necessary. The post mortem may reveal that the deceased died of natural causes in which case a certificate will be issued.

An inquest has to be held by the coroner in the case of every violent or unnatural death, such as an air or train crash or a fire. If the coroner feels that an inquest is necessary, a short formal inquest will be opened to record the death and identify the deceased. The inquest will then be adjourned. Where the coroner feels that disposal of the body will not prejudice his enquiries, he will issue the certificates required for a burial or cremation. The resumed inquest will take place later at a time and place to be notified by the coroner.

A Coroner's Court is a court of law and inquests are open to the public. It is not necessary for members of a family of the deceased to attend an inquest unless they are required as witnesses. A jury is summoned to an inquest in cases of industrial accidents, deaths in prison or police custody, traffic and air accidents and all cases where the circumstances of the death could have caused danger to the public. The jury is usually made up of seven people who are chosen in the same way as for any other court.

The Coroner's Court is not involved in apportioning blame or deciding on any criminal liabilities. The conclusions of the Coroner's Court indicate only the cause of death. They must be based on the evidence. In the case of a suspected suicide, if no conclusive evidence is available, there will be an open verdict.

The investigation of the coroner may take some time but the coroner can issue a coroner's certificate (similar to a doctor's certificate of death) to allow a funeral to take place before the conclusion of an inquest. A death certificate can only be issued after an inquest and the informant on that certificate will be the coroner.

An organisation named INQUEST (see Appendix II) helps families involved in dealing with coroners and inquests. It also publishes helpful information.

4

REGISTERING THE DEATH

Registration of a Death
All deaths must be registered with the Registrar of Births,
Deaths and Marriages. There is a statutory regulation in
the United Kingdom that, unless the coroner is involved,
registration must take place within five days of the actual
death (or within eight days in Scotland).

Who can Register a Death?
Registration of death is covered by the Births and Deaths
Registration Act 1953 and the reverse side of the doctor's
certificate of death shows who can register a death. This
information is divided into two parts. Any one of the persons
listed below can be legally responsible for registering a death
i.e. be the informant named on the death certificate.

A death in a house or public institution such as a
hospital can be registered by:

1. A relative of the deceased who was present at the
    death.
2. A relative of the deceased who was in attendance
    during the last illness.
3. A relative of the deceased who is living in or staying
    in the district where the death occurred.

4.   A person present at the death.
5.   The occupier if he has knowledge of the death. 'The
     occupier' can mean a hospital doctor, a governor of a
     prison, a superintendent of an institution or other
     chief resident officer.
6.   Any inmate if he knew of the death.
7.   The person 'causing the disposal of the body'. (The
     person responsible for the funeral.)

A death which doesn't occur in the places listed above or
where a dead body is found can be registered by:

1.   Any relative of the deceased who has knowledge of
     the particulars required to register a death.
2.   Any person present at the death.
3.   Any person who found the body.
4.   Any person in charge of the body.
5.   The person 'causing the disposal of the body'. (The
     person responsible for the funeral.)

If an inquest is held, the informant on the death certificate
will be the coroner.

If possible, the death should be registered by a relative
of the deceased since he is more likely to have knowledge
of the information requested by the Registrar for inclu-
sion in the certificate. Where this is not possible, because
there is no next of kin, the death may be registered by the
person responsible for arranging the funeral. In certain
circumstances the person in charge of an elderly persons'
residential home, where the deceased was resident, can
register a death. If you are unsure whether you can
register a death you should telephone the Registrar's
office for advice.

The death must be registered in the district where the
death occurred even if the person did not normally reside in

that area. It is usually necessary to make an appointment at the Registry in order to register the death. Often the hospital will make an appointment for you when they give you the doctor's certificate of death which must be handed to the Registrar. The hospital will know the address and opening times of the Registry. In some circumstances, registration can be done remotely. The Register Office can advise.

Doctor's Certificate
The doctor's certificate given to you will be in two parts. Hand the whole certificate to the Registrar; the Registrar will return one part to you.

What will the Registrar want to Know?
The Registrar will require certain information from the person registering the death. If it is available, it would be helpful to take a copy of the deceased's birth or marriage certificate and his passport, if he had one, to the Registrar's office when registering a death. It is important to check the register very carefully before the final signatures are added as it is very difficult, and in some cases impossible, to correct the information at a later date.

The questions asked will be:

1. Date and place of death.
2. Full name and sex of the deceased. If the deceased was known by a name other than that shown on his or her birth certificate, that name should also be given. If someone was registered at birth as 'Elizabeth' but was always known as 'Eliza' or 'Betty', or if 'Albert' was always known as 'Bert', both names should be given.
3. Date and place of birth of the deceased.
4. Occupation and usual address of the deceased. If the deceased was a retired person, the Registrar will ask for their main occupation or last employment.

5. Whether the deceased was single, married or widowed.
6. If a married woman, her maiden surname and any other names acquired through divorce or remarriage.
7. If a widow, the registrar will ask for the full names and last occupation of her deceased husband.
8. The name and address of the informant.
9. The relationship of the informant to the deceased.

Additional information shown on the certificate will be the cause of death. The Registrar will obtain this from the doctor's certificate. All this information is entered into a draft form and then into a computer. An official, printed certificate will be produced. The Registrar will sign and date the certificate.

The Registrar will provide one original death certificate and will ask if any further official copies are required. Official copy certificates will have to be sent to various interested people and companies (ordinary photocopied ones are not sufficient) and it would save time if a number of certificates are requested. If a third party, such as a relative has taken out an insurance on the life of the deceased, he will also need a copy of the death certificate. The Registrar will charge a fee for the death certificate and a small additional fee for each certified copy.

In case you require additional copies of the death certificate at a later date, ask the Registrar for the page number of the entry in the register.

Certificate for the Funeral Directors
The Registrar also issues what is known as a 'Green Certificate' which must be given to the funeral directors as soon as possible. This allows them to take possession of the deceased and to make arrangements for cremation or burial.

Notification for the Department of Social Services
If the person who has died was in receipt of a state pension
or state benefit, the Registrar will give you a signed form of
'Registration or Notification of Death'. You should complete Part One which is about the deceased and Part Two
which is about yourself. This form, together with any
pension or allowance books belonging to the deceased,
should then be sent to the local Benefits Agency of the
Social Services Department. The address of the DSS is
shown in local telephone directories under the title 'Benefits Agency'. You can obtain a free stamped and
addressed envelope from a local Post Office which you can
use to return the pension or allowance books. If you prefer,
you can hand the allowance books in at the Post Office
where the allowances were paid and the Post Office will
give you an official receipt. If the deceased was receiving
any benefits which were paid directly into a bank account,
there will be no pension or allowance books. The completed form of 'Registration and Notification of Death'
should be sent unaccompanied to the Benefits Agency.

5

LOOKING FOR THE WILL AND OTHER PAPERWORK

However distressing, it is essential to visit the home of the deceased to check what papers and documents have been left. These will be needed as soon as possible if you are to assess the situation and to be in a position to make immediate decisions. If you need to, take a friend or relative with you. It is always helpful to have someone to talk to. He may also have some ideas about where to look for things. Make sure you check handbags, suitcases, briefcases, shopping bags, shoe boxes, under cushions and in coat pockets. People, especially old people, store things in unusual places, particularly documents or belongings that they wish to preserve and if they feel vulnerable to burglaries.

It is not necessary at this stage to make any decisions about the general disposal of furniture and personal belongings – 'The Estate' – this can be done in a more relaxed atmosphere after the funeral (see Chapter 12). What you will be looking for is a will if there is one, instructions if there are any, insurance policies, jewellery, credit cards, vehicle documents (log books, insurance), premium bonds, share certificates, bank statements, building society account books, property deeds or mortgage information, rent book, lottery tickets, passport, cash and anything else that can help you in your task. It may be that if the deceased had a computer or an electronic address book or memo pad, all the information you need could be contained there. If you are uncertain how to use such items, there is probably a younger member of your family, who is used to computers, who could help you.

Finding a Will

In order for a will to be valid, it must be dated and signed by the testator (the person making the will). His signature must have been witnessed by two people (not beneficiaries or their spouses) who were present at the same time and who also signed the document. The full names and addresses of the witnesses must also be included in the will. If the will was drawn up by a solicitor, the witnesses were probably the solicitor and someone else in his office.

A will should name an executor who will be the person to carry out the wishes of the deceased. If you are not the named executor, then the will should be given to the executor. If no executor is named, the next of kin can apply for Letters of Administration.

If the will was made by the deceased without legal advice, the written instructions may not always be clear and may not reflect what the deceased person *meant* to say. The instructions in a valid will must be followed even if they do not accord with what the deceased really wished to say. He may have made verbal promises to bequeath some of his belongings to specific people but if there is a valid written will, and those bequests are not written in that will, then they should not be honoured. Anything not specifically disposed of in the will becomes part of the residue of the estate of the deceased.

This may seem insensitive and mercenary at the time, but if you are the one dealing with matters you will be responsible for the immediate payments such as the Registrar's fees and eventually the costs of the funeral. If there is a will you may not be a beneficiary, but funeral costs and ancillary costs are a first charge against the estate and will, of course, be paid out of the estate if there is sufficient. It will help you to know what is available. If there is nothing, then you must bear in mind that once you assume responsibility and give funeral instructions you will be responsible for payment of all necessary fees which could be substantial. Most people do leave some money somewhere and there is usually sufficient to pay the immediate costs.

It may be that the deceased, if elderly, has already given you some idea of how he would like to be dealt with when he died. Some people are very methodical and leave their affairs in good order. They may have told you where their personal documents are kept and what actions they wish you to take. Others give no thought to their death and you will have to make a systematic search of their home to find out whatever you can. You should look for letters to and from solicitors, possibly referring to a will, letters to and from a bank, the will itself and any correspondence which would help you. Some people pay in advance for a funeral and there will be a policy, contract or correspondence. This would be helpful since you would know which funeral directors to approach to deal with the funeral.

If there is a family grave where the deceased is to be buried it will be necessary to find the title deeds to the plot of land in the cemetery. If you cannot find them, you will need to prove by other means that the deceased is entitled to be buried in that plot. This point is dealt with in more detail in Chapter 7.

Cash on the Premises

Most people keep a reserve of cash in the house and you may come across some money in all sorts of places. Some elderly people say that they have no faith in banks and keep all their money at home. A distant relative of mine kept her money all over the house. There were £10, £20 and £50 notes under the carpet on the tread of each stair. Notes were spread under the carpets in the bedroom and living room, under the mattress in the bed and under cushions. Bundles of notes rolled up and secured by elastic bands were stuffed down the sides of armchairs, in plastic bags in the refrigerator and freezer, in drawers, handbags and coat pockets. Notes were even pinned into the folds of curtains. Eventually a total of over ten thousand pounds was discovered in the house. It is still not known for certain whether all the money was found. This was unusual, but it does happen. Many of the notes had been there for years and were out of date but they were accepted by a bank.

All this will take a great deal of time but it must be done if you are left with the responsibility of dealing with the estate.

6

WHOM TO TELL ABOUT THE DEATH

It will be a sad but necessary duty to inform people about the death. If they do not know already, the nearest relatives and family should be told as soon as possible. If there are any other family members, however distant (cousins, second cousins, aunts or uncles, whatever the relationship), they should also be informed. It may be that you know all the remaining family members and are in contact with them but it is also possible that you or the deceased have lost touch with some of the family.

Most people keep an address book and if you can find one kept by the deceased you can check on names, addresses and telephone numbers. The information may have been kept on a computer or electronic notepad. You will recognise the names of family members and some of the friends of the deceased.

If the deceased had an association with a local church or religious organisation such as a chapel or the Salvation Army, the minister or priest should be informed as soon as possible. This is particularly important if the deceased was a member of an ethnic religion where the rules relating to burial or cremation are very important.

If the deceased was employed, his employer should be informed of the death as soon as possible.

If the deceased was a member of a sports club or a professional association, such as a union, a local branch of the British Legion, Trades Council, or a member of the local Borough or Town Council, these institutions should be advised of the death.

How to Tell People

How you tell people of the death is sometimes a difficult decision to make and not to be taken lightly. If you know the people concerned you will be able to judge whether you should tell them by telephone, by letter, by e-mail, or personally by visiting them. If there are a number of telephone calls to make, this could be very time consuming. Ring at a time when you know they will be at home and in a relaxed frame of mind. It is not a good idea to telephone early in the morning when they are about to set off for work. It will usually do no harm to wait a few hours and to choose the right time to convey your message.

A simple statement is best (see Fig. 1 overleaf). The person you are calling will want to ask questions. You should answer as many as you can, but if you do not know the answers, say so.

If you are only able to reach an answer phone, it would be better to leave your name and number asking them to return your call as soon as possible, than to leave a message advising of the death.

When you need to contact people in other countries, there may be a time difference. The telephone operator can tell you what it is, or it may be shown somewhere in the telephone directory. Some personal diaries also show the different time zones.

In some cases it would be better to write, particularly where you do not know the person very well. A simple note

"This is [Give your name. Use your first name if you are well known to the person you are calling. If not, give your full name – first name and surname]. I am sorry to have to tell you that [Give the name of the deceased as known to the person you are calling – 'Aunt Jenny', 'Mrs Jenny Smith', 'Jenny Smith' or 'your cousin Jenny'] died this morning [or yesterday or this evening].

"I realise this is quite a shock, but I thought you would want to know as soon as possible. No funeral arrangements have been made yet. The arrangements have been left to me and I will contact you again as soon as I have more information. If you would like to talk to me later, my telephone number is 00000 00000 and I will be here every morning until 12 o'clock and most evenings after 7 o'clock."

Fig. 1. Telephone call advising of death

(Fig.2) is all that is necessary at this stage. Etiquette at one time would have required each note to be handwritten. This would be very nice but if you have a number of letters to write and have access to a computer, you could write one form of letter and print it with all the different names. You should, of course, sign each letter individually by hand. For someone on the Internet an e-mail can be sent. Letters abroad should be sent by the quickest possible method (e.g. fax) since the recipients may wish to attend the funeral and need to make travel arrangements.

Newspaper Obituary
You may feel that you do not know the names and addresses of all the friends and acquaintances of the deceased, in which case you could place an entry in the obituary column of the local newspaper. If the deceased had a wide range of friends, an entry in a national news-

---

Your address or the address
where you will be staying
until after the funeral

Tel: 00000 000000

date

Dear

I write to let you know that sadly ['Aunt Jenny', or 'Mrs Jenny Smith' or 'Jenny Smith' or 'Jenny'] died ['yesterday' or 'today'] after a short illness.

No funeral arrangements have been made yet. I will let you know as soon as I have any further information. If you would like to speak to me, my telephone number is 00000 000000 and I will be at that number every morning until 12 noon. Alternatively I will be there most evenings after 7 o'clock.

Yours sincerely

[sign the letter and also print your name under your signature]

Fig. 2. Letter advising of death

paper could also be considered. Perhaps he had lived in a different place for a considerable time and an entry in that local newspaper or the newspaper of the place in which he was born might also be a good idea.

The obituary could show the name of the deceased, the date of death and the time and place of the funeral once it is known (Fig.3 overleaf).

In order to avoid hoaxes, most newspapers will double check the information given, perhaps by ringing you back, to confirm that the details of the death are *bona fide*. You may wish to seek the advice and assistance of the funeral director in arranging newspaper announcements.

SMITH – Annie, aged 91 years, loved wife of the late Henry, died peacefully on July 2 after a short illness. Funeral service on Friday 8 July at 2.30 pm at Old Minster Church followed by cremation at Holm Crematorium. No flowers but donations to Cancer Research if so wished, c/o Wishley Funeral Directors, 21 Brown Street, Holm, Yorks, YO19 2AB.

SMITH – Annie suddenly at home on July 2nd. Daughter of the late Eliza and John Henry Carrington. Loving wife of the late Harry, dear sister of Mary and aunt of Sarah. Funeral at Holm Crematorium on Friday 8 July at 2.30 pm. Flowers may be sent to Wishley Funeral Directors, 21 Brown Street, Holm, or to Annie's home.

Fig. 3. Newspaper obituaries

Landlords

There are other people who must also be advised of the death. If the deceased owned the property in which he lived, there will be no landlord to inform. However, where the deceased was living in rented or leased accommodation, the landlord or lessor should be told. The tenancy would have ceased on the death and the landlord may have certain rules, particularly if it is a local authority or housing association.

In the case of my aunt who was living in a flat in sheltered accommodation, the local authority required one month's notice of vacating the property and the rent had to be paid. This was quite helpful as there was no rush to deal with the contents of the flat immediately. However, in a different situation, a flat had to be cleared within one week of the death, leaving very little time to make the necessary arrangements. An offer to pay rent to allow time was refused and the flat had to be cleared within the given time.

Some authorities stick to the rules however upsetting they may be – not only with regard to housing. There will be behaviour which you might find insensitive and distressing when you have to deal with pedantic people, but this comes in all walks of life and we have to deal with them as best we can without allowing ourselves to be too upset. However, if you think you are being dealt with unfairly, ask to see or speak to a more senior person or manager.

Family Doctor
The family doctor or General Practitioner may have been in attendance at the death or have been aware of a life-threatening illness of the deceased. The doctor or local Practice in which he or she is a partner should be informed of the death.

Pension Providers
If the deceased was retired and in receipt of a private pension or an employer's pension, the providers of the pension should be advised of his death. The pension provider will subsequently require to see a certified copy of the death certificate. The pension will probably cease at the date of death or there may be provisions for a surviving partner to receive a payment. There may be a lump sum payable on death.

Income Tax
If the deceased was a tax payer he will probably have tax documents amongst his papers. His Income Tax Office should be informed of the death and a certified copy of the death certificate sent to it. (Always request the return of any copy death certificates or Grant of Probate forms you send out.) If he was employed, his employers will be in possession of his tax records and will be able to advise the Income Tax Office of the death. You could request them to

do so. A certified copy of the death certificate should be given to the employers for this purpose.

Council Tax
The local authority dealing with Council Tax should be advised of the death, and any payment books returned to them, together with a certified copy of the death certificate.

Public Utilities, Telephone and TV Companies
The providers of utilities such as gas, electricity, water and telephone should be advised of the death; also the television rental or satellite or cable company, if the deceased rented a TV, video or other equipment. You will probably have found recent bills paid by the deceased for these services. They will give you the addresses and telephone numbers to contact and may give the relevant account number. If not, look up the telephone numbers in the telephone directory.

Most services will accept the information of a death by telephone and will request a follow up letter of confirmation. Some will require a copy of the death certificate to accompany the letter.

I know of one case where a person died over ten years ago and despite numerous letters and telephone calls, bills still arrive addressed to the deceased. They are paid regularly by his widow. Fortunately she finds this irritating rather than distressing.

In most cases, when requested, the utilities will continue to supply the services to the property until it is vacated. Advise them of the date when the services should be discontinued and ask for a bill up to that date.

You will find it very useful to continue to have the use of the telephone if there is one. You can inform the telephone company of the death, requesting that the line be left in use. When the property is to be vacated, the telephone line can be discontinued or passed on to the new occupants, and the company will send a bill calculated up to that date.

Or else you can wait until you are ready to close up the property and then advise them, requesting a bill to the date of vacating the property.

You should request all bills to be addressed to "The Estate" of the deceased. You can ask for the bills and accounts to be sent to you, provided you are dealing with the estate. If there is a solicitor involved they could be sent to the solicitor.

Banks and Building Societies

Where you have found evidence of any bank or building society accounts or a National Savings Account Book or other savings accounts, inform these organisations in writing, sending them a copy of the death certificate. All monetary accounts will be frozen as from the date of death and all direct debits and standing orders cancelled.

If any cheques have been paid by the deceased but not presented for payment before the date of death, those cheques would not be met. The amounts that would have been paid should be shown in the accounts of the estate as debts due from the estate.

Joint Accounts

If the deceased held any joint bank, mortgage or savings accounts, then those accounts will not be frozen and can be operated by the surviving partner. However, the surviving partner still, of course, has to inform the bank of the death, and the value of the deceased's half share is part of the estate.

Recipients of Regular Outgoings

Where the deceased had a current account with a bank, the recent statements and cheque book stubs could give you some indication of any regular weekly or monthly payments made by the deceased which may indicate some ongoing debts. The recipients of those payments should be advised of the death. Any debts due up to the date of death will be a charge on the estate of the deceased. If you cannot initially find the recipients' addresses, demands for payment will eventually be sent by mail and you can then advise them of the death.

Mortgages

If the deceased owned any land or property and the property was mortgaged, then the mortgage company or lender must be advised. Any mortgage repayments which were made regularly by direct debit or through a bank account will cease as from the date of death unless there was a joint mortgage account. Adjustments to the total amount due when the mortgage is repaid will take into account that the regular payments ceased on the death.

Car and Vehicle Insurance

Insurance cover on a vehicle insured by the deceased stops immediately at the date of death. The insurance company concerned should be informed immediately of the death. They will probably offer to arrange a transfer of the insurance cover to an executor or a family member. Most personal car insurance policies have a clause enabling the insured to drive a car which is not his own with the minimum legal cover, and this facility can enable an executor to move a car to a safer/better place or send it for sale later. Check your own policy.

Insurance Companies

Many people insure their homes and the contents and the insurance is dependent upon the home being occupied. If you have found evidence of any such insurance you should inform the insurance company of the death and request that the insurance be maintained until the property is vacated and the estate has been dealt with. If the current insurers will not agree to this, you should consider taking out a separate insurance policy to cover the premises and contents for a short time.

Credit Cards
For any credit cards in the name of the deceased (Visa, Mastercard, American Express, etc, or any store credit cards), the companies should be advised of the death. The account numbers are shown on the credit cards and should be quoted. A telephone call initially will suffice, followed by written confirmation with a certified copy of the death certificate and the actual cards (cut up so no one else can use them) sent to the company. A request for a statement of account as at the date of death should be made.

   If the deceased was the first-named account holder of a joint credit card account, on his death the company may suspend the credit card account, thereby preventing the secondary account holder (normally his spouse) from using the credit card. In that event, the surviving partner will need to set up his or her own new account. Where there are two account holders, the first-named holder is responsible for payment. If the first-named holder dies, any amounts due are a charge on the estate of the deceased.

7

BURIAL OR CREMATION?

Burial

There are now usually more cremations than burials. However, in parts of Scotland and Wales burials still outnumber cremations. This is probably because there is more land available and fewer crematoria have been built. A few years ago there was only one crematorium in Wales but now there are over fifteen.

A decision for a burial gives rise to a number of points requiring consideration. The first is where the burial is to take place; usually in a cemetery. In London there is only one churchyard where burials now occur and that is a churchyard of a Catholic Church. In the mid-nineteenth century, churchyards in large cities became so overcrowded that they had to be closed. Private cemeteries and graveyards were opened but many have since disappeared due to the lack of upkeep. In most cases, burials now take place in local corporation or company owned cemeteries. The funeral directors you choose will tell you where they have facilities for burial. They may offer a selection of several local cemeteries or they may have only one that they use.

In rural areas, burials can usually be arranged in a local churchyard.

Burial Outside a Cemetery
It is a little known fact that a person can be buried almost anywhere that is considered suitable, provided permission is obtained from the owners of the land. A person can elect to be buried in his own garden. But this is not a simple matter and certain formalities have to be observed.

If a burial is to take place outside a recognised venue, it is necessary first to obtain a certificate of disposal from the local Registrar of Births, Deaths and Marriages. If the death has been dealt with by a coroner, then the coroner's office can provide a similar certificate. Such a certificate is required as a protection both for the burial and for the person arranging it. It is certain that murderers who bury their victims in cellars, back gardens or distant woods and fields, do not apply for certificates of disposal! However, any legitimate burial is safe from inquisitive neighbours or police enquiries if a certificate of disposal can be produced.

If the deceased has requested burial in his own garden, it is necessary to consider whether this request can be adhered to. It may be that the property will have to be sold at some time and the presence of a body buried in the garden might become a deterrent for purchasers. Also once the property has been sold, unless arrangements are made at the time of the sale and it is written into the conveyance of sale, it would not easily be possible to visit the grave if someone wished to do so. Requests made by the deceased in their lifetime should be honoured after their death if at all possible, but do not feel disloyal if this is not always a practical proposition and cannot be followed.

It is possible for the exhumation of a coffin and removal to another venue if required. This is a costly process and is time consuming, since it cannot take place during normal burial hours. The cost at present could be as high as £10,000 for each coffin. It is also governed by health and safety rules and a health and environmental official would have to be present. One young lady who was moving away to another district wished to take her deceased parents with her. The exhumation was arranged and the coffins were removed and transferred and buried in another cemetery.

Another point to consider when arranging a burial outside the normal venues is that the environmental health department of the local authority should be consulted. The local authority have the power to prevent a burial where it might contaminate or pollute water supplies.

It is becoming popular to arrange for a burial in a forest or woodland area. There are over 100 woodland burial grounds now established in the UK. At these burials, cardboard coffins tend to be used and, instead of headstones, trees may be planted to commemorate the dead. For more information, contact The Natural Death Centre (details in Appendix II).

Where it is really desired that the burial take place outside a cemetery the funeral director will be able to advise you on what possibilities are available. Any moves away from the normal would, of course, involve more cost.

Opening an Existing Grave
Sometimes a married couple or a whole family wish to be buried together in the same grave. When one of the family has already died and is buried, it will be necessary to arrange for the grave to be opened in order for subsequent burials to take place. Usually the funeral directors will make the necessary arrangements with the cemetery for a grave to be opened. Generally a grave holds up to four people.

Deeds of Ownership of a Grave
It is necessary to prove the ownership of a grave when it is to be opened for an additional burial and the deeds to the burial plot will probably be held by someone in the family or you may have found them in the home of the deceased.

The deeds should be handed to the funeral directors who will pass them to the manager of the cemetery, together with the statutory forms that have to be completed. These will be carefully checked against the records held by the cemetery and an entry made on the deeds showing the new burial. Arrangements will be made for the opening of the existing grave and the removal of any headstone or fixed memorial which will be replaced after the additional burial. The deeds will then be returned to the funeral directors who will pass them back to the person dealing with the funeral.

If the deeds cannot be found, the cemetery will have all the necessary records and someone arranging a burial will have to sign a form of indemnity to the effect that the person being buried has the right to be buried in that plot. This indemnifies the cemetery against any claims that might be made in the future that the person buried has no right to be in that grave.

It is allowed, and when a family agrees, anyone can be buried in a family grave even if not a member of the family. Provided the deeds of a plot are available and ownership is proved, the owner can request that a friend or anyone else be buried in that plot. If you are the owner of a burial plot and you know that there are no family members remaining who wish to be buried there, you can bury anyone you like in that plot. As usual, the burial will be entered on the deeds.

Charges are made by the cemetery for the upkeep of the cemetery grounds around burial plots. The upkeep of the actual burial plot is the responsibility of the owner of the plot.

Burial at Sea
Burial at sea can be arranged but is very costly. A licence under the Food and Environmental Protection Act is necessary, but the government will accept written notification from a funeral director in place of this licence. An

application must be made to the coroner for permission to remove a body from his jurisdiction for burial at sea. There are a few designated locations for burials at sea. This is another area where it will be necessary for professional funeral directors to make all the necessary legal and formal arrangements.

Headstones and Memorials
An existing headstone at a grave will be removed to allow a second or later burial to take place in that grave. Once the grave has settled, which takes several months, the headstone can be replaced. In the case of a new grave a new headstone can be erected.

In earlier times very large headstones and memorials in fantastic shapes were erected. In the famous Highgate cemetery, one of the memorials is in the shape of a grand piano, another has carved lions. Columns and angels were very popular and perhaps the most well known is the memorial of Karl Marx which is an enormous sculpture of his head. In country churchyards many memorials showing angels and children can be seen.

These days due to the lack of space and for ease of maintenance, most cemeteries and churchyards have restrictions relating to the size and type of headstone that may be erected. Most cemeteries will allow what are known as lawn graves with no surrounds but only a headstone. The headstones of the graves are in line with each other. This enables the authorities to keep the cemetery grounds in good order. Some have restrictions as to the wording that may be carved on the headstone. The deceased may at some time have expressed a request as to what is to be shown on his or her headstone. Normally the full name of the deceased together with his dates of birth and death are shown. If the deceased was married, the name of the spouse might also be shown. Suitable wording

of a memorial can be added. The names of children or
parents can also be included. (See Fig.4.)

"Sacred to the memory of HENRY SMITH who died
on 2nd July 2000 aged 69 years.
Also
in loving memory of his wife JENNY SMITH who
died on 5th May 2001 aged 70 years."

Or

"HENRY SMITH
1930 – 2000
Husband of Jenny, father of Mary, John and Carol.
In our memory forever."

Or

"HENRY SMITH
born in this parish 1930
beloved husband of Jenny
died 2nd July 2000
also
JENNY SMITH his wife
born in the parish of Kensal 1931
daughter of George and Katherine Howes
mother of Mary, John and Carol.
Together at rest in the hands of the Lord."

Fig. 4. Memorial inscriptions

On an existing headstone additional carving may be
required. You may not know who did the original work.
The cemetery will have records of monumental masons
who erect headstones in their cemetery and will probably

be able to tell you who was responsible for the original work. It would be advisable to use the same mason if possible so that the new wording matches the original as closely as possible.

Usually a small permanent vase for flowers can also be placed on the grave. These arrangements can be made with the cemetery manager after the funeral has taken place. The cemetery manager will be able to advise the type of memorial vase which is allowed and can be supplied as part of the cemetery services.

There is usually a 'Book of Remembrance' at the cemetery in which the name of the deceased can be written. Some people prefer the entry to be made showing the date of birth and some prefer the date of death. The pages of the book are turned daily so that the name and memorial to the deceased will be there for all to read on the chosen date each year.

Cremation
Cremation is now the method most frequently chosen when a funeral has to be arranged. It is considered to be more hygienic and is less costly than a burial. In the last forty years there has been a change from 70% burials to 70% cremations. Cremation is now acceptable for the Catholic community and is becoming more popular.

In order for a body to be cremated it is necessary for a second medical practitioner to examine the deceased and then countersign the 'green certificate' (obtained from the Registrar at the time the death certificate was issued). All funeral directors will arrange for this to be done. The person arranging the cremation has to sign a declaration that there are no objections to a cremation. Even if the deceased person has indicated that he or she wishes to be cremated, it is a good idea to discuss this aspect of the arrangements with any members of the family who may be interested. If someone objects after a cremation, this may cause difficulties for the person arranging the funeral. It is better to be safe than sorry and to avoid any disruptions to the ceremony or recriminations afterwards.

It is possible to arrange to see the actual cremation if you should wish to do so. Some religions make it mandatory for the immediate members of the family to see the body consumed and crematoria will make such arrangements where required. A few members of the family are allowed to watch as the coffin is charged into the cremator.

Each crematorium keeps a register of cremations and a certified copy of the entry in that register can be requested on payment of a fee.

The Ashes

Although some people have expressed doubts concerning the authenticity of the ashes which are handed to the family after a cremation, any crematorium will confirm that each person is separately cremated. You can be assured that, barring an unusual mistake, the ashes you receive are those of the person whose cremation you have arranged. The cremator is totally cleared after each cremation before another coffin can be dealt with.

All coffins whether for burial or cremation have to have a plaque on them showing the name of the deceased. The plaque is made of a combustible material suitable for burning in the cremator. The coffin and contents are consumed by the heat and whatever remains are the main bones. These are crushed in a cremulator which is a revolving drum with ball bearings in it and these form the ashes that you receive.

Almost anything can be done with the ashes. If an immediate decision cannot be made, the crematorium will store the ashes on payment of a monthly fee until such time as they are moved. The funeral directors will also store the ashes for a short time if requested to do so. The ashes can be scattered, buried or kept by a member of the family or a friend. There is usually a garden of remembrance or a woodland area at the crematorium where the ashes may be scattered. A small tree or rose bush can be planted and the ashes scattered there with a name plaque beside the tree. If a tree or bush is planted, do remember that it will have to be looked after by someone. A member of the family or a friend may wish to assume this responsibility or the crematorium managers can maintain the tree or bush for a yearly fee. This information can be obtained from the crematorium or the funeral directors.

Provided permission is obtained from the land owner, ashes can be scattered anywhere. Some people express a wish for their ashes to be scattered in certain places or you may wish to scatter them somewhere significant to the dead person.

When a decision has been reached, if the ashes are to be scattered, a clergyman or religious representative could be asked to be present to conduct a short ceremony and to say a prayer if that is what the deceased would have wanted.

A request that the ashes of a lady, who was 91 years old when she died and who had been a lifelong supporter of a London football club, be scattered on the football ground was refused. However, in a small ceremony her ashes were buried under the football pitch and will remain there for as long as the team plays. Football and cricket fans have had their ashes scattered over their teams' grounds. If the deceased had a particular sporting interest it is worth enquiring whether their ashes can be scattered at the sporting venue; perhaps a favourite racecourse or rugby ground.

Ashes can also be scattered at sea – a favourite idea. If requested a local RNLI lifeboat might be requested to scatter the ashes when out on an exercise.

The members of a family may wish to hire a boat and take the ashes to a favourite spot near where happy holidays had been spent. Local boats can be hired so that someone with a knowledge of local tides and winds can give advice. Flowers can be thrown onto the sea at the same time as the ashes. A well known place for scattering ashes is Land's End where the local boat owners will take a group of people out to sea for that purpose.

One young person whose mother died has her mother's ashes in a specially designed casket, which incorporates a photograph of her mother, on a small table at home. Flowers are always beside the casket and she remembers her mother's birthday and also Mothers' Day with a card placed beside the ashes.

The disposal of the ashes of a loved one is a matter for thought since, once scattered, there will be nothing tangible left as there is with a grave. There really is no limit as to what can happen to the ashes and many imaginative things can be done.

There are a number of books both novels and biographies which refer to the scattering of ashes. One novel referring to the experiences of a group travelling to scatter ashes won a Booker Prize. Without being disrespectful the book was highly entertaining. It can sometimes be comforting to know that others have experiences similar to your own and that you are not the only one to find humour in unexpected situations.

8

INITIAL FUNERAL
ARRANGEMENTS

Arranging a funeral is the last thing we can do for the deceased so we must do our best to give him a good one. A good funeral does *not* mean an expensive or elaborate funeral, but a sensitive and caring occasion. It also helps the family and friends who are left to grieve.

Pre-paid Funerals

More and more people these days are arranging with a funeral director, through an insurance company, or with the advice of a charity such as Help the Aged, to pay in advance for their own funeral. If such an arrangement has been made, the person concerned will usually tell someone – a friend or family member – what he has done. If not, you may find correspondence, or possibly an insurance policy, amongst the deceased's papers. You will then know the name and address of the designated funeral director (which may not be local) and the value of the policy or pre-paid funeral. There should be no further money to pay, except for any additional requirements not covered by the policy, such as increasing the number of cars required and choosing a more elaborate service.

Choosing a Funeral Director

You do not need to wait for the necessary certificate (the 'green certificate') before preliminary arrangements for a funeral can be made. You can visit a funeral director to fix the date and time.

In the past, funeral directors were part of the local community, known to most families. Often by tradition the local builder and joiner was also the funeral director. In recent years, many small independent funeral directors have joined into a corporate group or been taken over by a larger company, so that their staff are moved around and have less opportunity to get to know the local population. This can make it difficult to choose a funeral director since arranging a funeral is such a personal matter.

Most funeral directors belong to a trade association such as the National Association of Funeral Directors or the Society of Allied and Independent Funeral Directors. These associations can advise you of the names of local companies. If you choose one which is affiliated to an association, it should provide a certain standard of service. There is also the Funeral Ombudsman Scheme which can offer some protection.

Details of how to arrange a funeral without using a funeral director are given at the end of this chapter, on page 64.

The deceased may have left instructions naming the specific funeral directors to be approached or there may be a local funeral director who has been responsible for the funeral arrangements for other members of the family. If you have no instructions and do not know any local funeral directors, you can find the names and addresses of some in the yellow pages of the telephone directory or in the local newspaper or even on the Internet.

Alternatively, you can enquire at the Registrar's office when registering the death. Registrars' offices usually have a list of names of local funeral directors and some will have business cards of funeral directors available. They are not allowed to make recommendations, but they may give assistance by displaying the names of funeral directors.

You may wish to visit more than one funeral director or speak to several local funeral directors on the telephone in order to compare prices and find out which one you think will offer you the best service. Some funeral directors may agree a discount for payment of the full amount upfront.

Once a funeral director has been chosen, you can either telephone to make an appointment or go directly to their office. You will usually find a comfortable room awaiting you and a sympathetic and professional person to help you and deal with all your enquiries. If you feel happier taking someone with you, such as a member of the family or a friend, it might be helpful. If you prefer, the funeral director will send a representative to see you at the deceased's or your own home.

Funeral directors will have brochures and pictures available. Most will offer a 'basic funeral', and a typical specification would be as follows:

Provision of the funeral director's services.
Attending to all of the necessary arrangements.
Provision of the necessary staff.
Provision of a coffin suitable for the purpose of
    cremation or of burial.
Transfer of the deceased from the place of death (at least
    ten running miles allowed) in normal working hours.
Care of the deceased prior to the funeral.
Provision of a hearse to the nearest crematorium or
    cemetery.
Burial may be specified as opposed to/instead of
    cremation where this is locally available.

A 'basic funeral' does not normally include embalming, viewing the deceased, or provision of limousines, or fees or disbursements paid out to others. These, and probably more, may be required and will add to the cost.

Paying for a Funeral
When you visit the funeral directors you should know whether there will be sufficient money in the estate to pay for the funeral. If not, you will have to decide whether you wish to pay for it yourself or whether there are any family members of the deceased who may wish to do so. The total costs will depend upon what detailed services are required, such as the type of coffin and how many cars are needed.

If there is no money to pay for a funeral, you should tell the funeral directors and they will advise you how to apply to the Health Authority or Local Authority to arrange a funeral (see overleaf).

Funeral directors, once instructed, normally pay for all expenses, such as additional payments to doctors, clergy, crematorium and cemetery fees, and they will give details of those payments in their final account. They also pay for other necessary disbursements if ordered, such as death notices in newspapers, printing, and catering.

Reputable funeral directors will give you a written estimate of the total costs involved, taking into account all the services you require.

Once you have decided upon a particular firm to conduct the funeral, you will need to pay a deposit. The funeral directors have to pay for doctors' certificates, ministers' fees and most cemetery and crematorium fees in advance. Many funeral directors accept payment by recognised credit cards, such as Visa or Mastercard.

When you are sure that there is sufficient money in the estate to pay for the funeral, or you know that the deceased had a bank account, the funeral directors may be happy to send the final invoice directly to the bank for payment. The bank should be advised and requested to pay the invoice direct; it may make a charge for this service. The final invoice is usually submitted for payment about two weeks after the funeral.

Most funeral directors will come to an arrangement concerning the payment of the invoice if the money is not immediately available but it is best to sort out all the financial details at the outset.

Social Fund

There is no death grant payable by the Social Services, but the surviving partner may be eligible for a Social Fund Payment, though this will probably not pay the whole cost of the funeral. In order to qualify for a payment, either the deceased or the surviving partner should be in receipt of such State Benefits as Income Support, Council Tax Benefit, Family Credit, Housing Benefit or Disability Benefit at the date of death. To make a claim for assistance, apply to the Department of Social Services. Information concerning this is available on Form SF200 issued by the DSS.

Funeral Payments by the Health Authority or the Local Authority

If a person dies in hospital and there is insufficient money to pay for a funeral, the hospital administrator will organise and pay for a simple 'contract' funeral through the local funeral directors who act for them. Otherwise this task falls to the Local Authority. They will usually arrange for a cremation, not a burial, since a cremation is less costly. This is a very simple funeral, and relatives get little say in the arrangements.

Decisions about the Funeral

The funeral directors will need to ask a number of questions when you visit them initially but will not necessarily go into detail for the final arrangements.

The first decision you will have to make is whether you require a burial or a cremation. A burial is usually more costly than a cremation because there is a plot of land involved. For more information, see Chapter 7.

If the deceased attended a place of worship, then you will probably want to arrange for his local vicar or priest to conduct the funeral service. In that event, you need to consult with him at an early stage and decide whether there is to be a separate religious ceremony in the deceased's local church or chapel (with music and perhaps a choir and with the deceased's favourite hymns being sung) or whether the service at the crematorium or cemetery will be sufficient. A church service would normally be followed by a shorter service of committal at the crematorium or cemetery chapel and should be timed appropriately.

If the deceased was not a churchgoer, you may prefer not to have a traditional religious service at all, feeling that the service might be rather impersonal as the local clergyman would know little about his life. Anyone (a member of the family or a close friend) can organise what happens at a funeral if a religious service is not required. The crematorium manager or funeral director will advise and assist if requested to do so.

A friend or members of the family can speak at the service making it more personal. A funeral service is a farewell and is also an opportunity for a celebration of the life of the deceased. Although a sad occasion, it does not necessarily have to be depressing or morbid. The atmosphere should always be respectful. The staff at the crematorium or cemetery and the staff of the funeral directors will always show respect and help to set the tone of the proceedings. Professional funeral assistants feel that the mourners should have whatever kind of service and attention they require, but they do prefer not to have very noisy or disrespectful behaviour. The tone of the proceedings can be decided by the type of service and the music.

Choice of Coffin

The funeral director will offer a choice of coffin, possibly a casket. The more elaborate it is, the more costly it will be. The material from which it is constructed will, of course, affect the price. The majority of coffins today are made out of chipboard with a wood veneer face. A casket is a different shape from a coffin. It is more elaborate and has more decoration. It could be constructed of heavier wood with carving and ornamentation.

All coffins, whether for a burial or a cremation, will have a plaque on them, giving the name of the deceased. Most crematoria insist that it also shows the date of death and age. This ensures that the correct person is being cremated, with the correct family in attendance. On occasions there have been mix-ups, but these are very rare, and the crematorium staff are very careful to make sure that everything is correctly carried out.

The funeral directors will ask you whether you have any special instructions with regard to how the deceased should be clothed. Do you wish him to wear his own clothes or a simple gown provided by them? If you decide upon the former, you will have to choose which clothes and take them to the funeral directors' office. You may know the deceased's favourite suit or dress. If he had a particular hobby or interest which involved a uniform or special clothes, you may think it suitable for them to be worn. A cricketer, for instance, might wear his club blazer; a member of the armed forces might, if it is allowed, wear his uniform; or an actor might wear his favourite costume.

You will also have to decide whether he is to wear any jewellery. A married person might wear his wedding ring, for instance. A man might wear a personalised or initial

ring or a chain or medallion that he has always worn. A
crucifix on a chain is something to consider or a rosary if
the deceased was a Catholic. The deceased's priest can
advise on this point. Remember, though, that any jewellery
worn by the deceased will disintegrate during a cremation.

The Hearse

The coffin will be carried in a hearse. This is normally a
specially adapted black limousine car with long side-
windows so that the coffin, and any flowers, can be seen.
Usually a very modern car is used but very old Rolls-
Royces are popular for upmarket funerals.

Where other forms of transport are required, perhaps
because of family tradition, such as a horse-drawn hearse,
this can be discussed with the funeral directors who will let
you know what is available. Arrangements for something
other than a standard car can be made but will be more
costly.

Cars for the Mourners

The cars used by funeral directors can normally carry six
people. On your initial visit to the funeral directors you
may not know exactly how many cars are required as it will
depend on the number of close family members attending
the funeral who will require transport. However, as soon as
you do know, inform the funeral directors. Make arrangements with them if you wish people to be brought back to
the deceased's home or to a reception elsewhere. Additional
cars required at short notice can usually be provided. If
necessary, ask the funeral directors to supply written travel
instructions to the funeral venue for those who will be
following in their own cars.

Printing

The funeral directors can supply a number of different
printed items if required. In particular, once the details of

the funeral service have been decided, they can provide a personal printed Order of Service. The front cover can show the name of the deceased, the years of his birth and death, together with the date, time and place of the funeral. Cemetery chapels and crematoria usually provide leaflets or books containing the standard Order of Service as part of their facilities.

If it is to be a religious service, the Order can contain details of the hymns to be sung with the verses, Bible readings and addresses, and the music to be played. If there is no religious service, it can contain the names of the speakers and details of the music, and perhaps one of the deceased's favourite passages from literature.

A printed Order of Service can be as elaborate or as simple as required. It can have a heavily embossed cover with cords or tassels or it can be a simple one-page sheet. A photograph of the deceased can be incorporated if required. The funeral directors will have samples available.

The Order of Service can be handed to the mourners as they arrive, either by an assistant of the funeral directors at the crematorium or cemetery chapel, or by a churchwarden or friend of the family at the local church. It is a helpful guide and provides a memorial for those attending the funeral.

Floral Tributes
The funeral directors are usually able to recommend a local florist and often have brochures showing the designs that are available. When the time and date of the funeral are agreed, they will advise you when the flowers should be delivered to them.

Large formal floral arrangements are usually provided inside the crematorium or chapel and the cost of this is included in the fees, but if you require some special floral decorations you can ask the funeral directors to deal with them. The flowers can then be left in the chapel for other funerals or removed at your direction.

If a service is to be held in a church and floral arrangements are required, this can be discussed with the clergyman when arranging the details of the funeral service. Many churches have floral arrangements provided by volunteer church workers and the clergyman might put you in touch with someone who is in charge of the flower arrangements for the church so that you can discuss this with them. You can pay for additional flowers or, if you are happy to allow the church to provide the flowers, you could make a donation to their flower fund.

During one cremation that I attended, the family arranged for two large containers of loose, mixed flowers to be placed either side of the coffin. The coffin remained in view during the service and mourners were invited to place flowers from the containers on the coffin as they left. Many of the mourners appreciated being able to make a final gesture of farewell and stood by the coffin for a short time after placing the flowers.

If flowers have been requested, ask the funeral directors to collect the notes of condolence from the tributes so that the people sending the flowers can be thanked formally later on. The floral tributes will be displayed outside the chapel for the mourners to see after a cremation or on a grave after the burial has taken place. Time will be allowed for this before the cars take the mourners home. Funeral floral tributes are not usually acceptable to hospitals, hospices or nursing homes, since such places would have too many; and funeral flowers are not always ideal for other uses either. It does seem a pity for all those beautiful flowers to be left but, if asked, the funeral directors will arrange for the flowers to remain in the chapel.

If there are to be no flowers, the funeral directors should be told. Donations to a charity, possibly a favourite charity of the deceased, can be requested. Tell friends and family who wish to donate, the name and address of the charity or where donations can be sent. Also give the funeral directors this information so that they can pass it on to anyone making enquiries. They may be prepared to accept the donations at their office.

Chapel of Rest

When you have discussed the matter of the funeral and are satisfied that you wish to use the services of a particular funeral director, you can hand to the funeral assistant the 'green certificate'. If the death was in hospital, you may well have the release note (removal order) from the hospital, which you have to sign so that the funeral director can gain possession of the deceased. These documents will enable the funeral directors to collect the deceased and bring him to their own Chapel of Rest. Arrangements can then be made for friends and family to visit the body if they wish to do so. Visits must be made by appointment and the funeral directors will advise you of the times when visits can be made, and the time and date of the final visit immediately prior to the funeral. If necessary, they will arrange for a visit outside their normal hours of business.

Agreeing a Date and Time

The funeral directors will give you a choice of dates, times and venues for the funeral. Some crematoria only work on certain days of the week which means that all cremations have to take place on those days. The length of time allowed for a service is usually sufficient, but it may be restricted by the fact that other funerals will follow. The funeral directors will tell you roughly how long a service may take. If you have planned a service and know its length, timings can be adjusted.

Often, however, you may not wish to make a decision on these matters at the initial meeting as you may need to confer with other members of the family. The funeral directors will advise how soon they need to know the details of your choice.

Ethnic Religions
Where the person who has died is of an ethnic religion, there may be specific funeral directors who deal with such funeral arrangements. The Registrar of Deaths can advise where you can contact a funeral director for a religion other than the Church of England, or the hospital manager or chaplain, or another local funeral director may have this information. The local cemetery or crematorium manager can also advise regarding the requirements for ethnic funerals and will know the names and addresses of funeral directors. Alternatively, you can contact the local chapel, mosque or synagogue for assistance; most religious organisations give their numbers in the local telephone directory.

Jewish Religion
According to the requirements of the Jewish religion, Jewish funerals have to take place as near as possible within 48 hours of the death. Specialist funeral directors are aware of this and are able to deal with matters. They will make all the necessary arrangements. Jewish funerals take place in Jewish cemeteries and it is mostly men who attend. If women are present, they are usually close relatives and remain separate from the men at the service. At the burial, the mourners are expected to participate in the act of burial.

Hindu Religion
It is a requirement of the Hindu religion that the deceased be cremated. Members of the family need to be present at

the actual cremation and this can be arranged. Crematoria will normally only allow a small number of mourners in the cremator room.

Muslim Religion
Muslims usually appoint one person in a locality to deal with the funeral arrangements. Burials must take place within 24 hours of the death and traditionally bodies are wrapped in a plain sheet with no coffin. However, the regulations at most cemeteries require a coffin. Muslims are not cremated but are buried in separate graves. This, of course, will make the funeral more costly since a separate plot has to be purchased for each person, whereas in most cemeteries it is normal to make graves available for four people.

Quakers
Quaker funerals are usually very simple but are arranged in accordance with the expressed wishes of the deceased or their family. They can be either a burial or a cremation. There are some Quaker burial grounds, and information can be obtained from their main Meeting House. The funeral service is conducted by an Elder and is mostly a silent gathering but anyone who wishes to can speak. The service ends with the shaking of hands.

Funeral with no Funeral Director
It is not necessary to use the services of a funeral director if you do not wish to do so. Burial or cremation can be arranged directly with the cemetery, crematorium or place where the burial is to take place. However, there are a number of regulations which have to be followed, including the completion of statutory forms, required before a burial or cremation can take place.

The material from which the coffin is constructed is also important. For a cremation, certain materials are not suitable because of the Environmental Protection Act and the rules regarding smoke emission. The crematorium has monitoring equipment to prevent such pollution and any incorrect material would cause great problems. The coffin handles and decorations – known as the 'coffin furniture' – are never made of brass. If they were made of metal, they would have to be removed by the crematorium staff before the actual cremation could take place.

Who is to construct the coffin and where the deceased can be lodged while awaiting the funeral can also be a problem and could raise difficulties where the matter is to be dealt with privately and not through a recognised funeral director. If there is room available at a mortuary, the deceased can be lodged there until funeral arrangements are made.

If you approach the cemetery or crematorium directly they will deal with the funeral. They will probably suggest that you use the services of an experienced funeral director because it makes the whole matter easier to deal with both for you and for them, but they will not insist and will help as much as they are able.

A gentleman who was a carpenter prepared his own coffin and left explicit instructions regarding his cremation. His family, after making arrangements directly with the crematorium, brought the deceased to the crematorium in the back of the company van.

Any method of transport can be used to bring the deceased to the crematorium or cemetery, but the staff prefer a funeral to be dealt with by a professional funeral director since 'the back of a lorry' or 'in an estate car' is considered by them to be undignified.

The Natural Death Centre in London (see Appendix II) is a charity which helps families to plan environmentally friendly funerals with the minimum of expense.

9

FINAL FUNERAL ARRANGEMENTS

Seating at the Funeral Service

Some thought should be given to the seating arrangement at the service. Usually the family members sit in the front on the right-hand side nearest to the coffin. The other principal mourners, including, if they are to be present, any local dignitaries, representatives from employers, clubs, organisations and charities supported by the deceased, should be seated at the front on the left-hand side. Seats could be reserved for the principal mourners. Other mourners can fill places as they arrive. A member of the funeral directors' staff will be in the chapel to help but if you think it will be easier, ask the funeral directors to provide someone to act specifically as an usher inside the chapel. If the service is in a church, the clergyman might suggest the order of seating or ask a church warden to be in attendance to help and to direct the mourners to their seats.

Route for the Cortège

If the deceased was employed or belonged to a club, church or chapel, the funeral cortège can be taken past where he worked or stop outside for his friends and colleagues to say goodbye and pay their respects. This should be arranged with the funeral directors as they will normally have a regular route that they follow to the funeral venue. They may need to make arrangements in the light of traffic regulations and conditions.

At the appropriate time, the hearse carrying the deceased can be brought to his home and the mourners go from there, or the hearse can be met at the cemetery or at a church or chapel if there is to be service before the final act of farewell. In some parts of the country it is felt that the body in the hearse should be taken to the cemetery or church from the home in order to allow neighbours and friends to pay their last respects.

In the case of my aunt, who lived in sheltered accommodation, I was reluctant to allow the funeral to leave from her home in case it upset her elderly neighbours. However, I was asked specifically to allow the hearse to visit her home. All her friends and neighbours came out into the courtyard to bid her farewell and to give their floral tributes personally to the funeral directors so that they could see them placed on the hearse.

When the hearse moves off, it will travel slowly through the neighbourhood, sometimes with one of the funeral attendants walking alongside, so that local friends and neighbours can pay their respects. In rural districts it may be arranged that all the mourners follow the hearse on foot and walk to the burial.

You will be asked whether the funeral directors are required to be pall bearers and carry the coffin into the chapel or church, or whether friends or family members wish to do this. The funeral directors will explain what can be done. Perhaps friends and family prefer to meet the coffin at the cemetery gates and carry the coffin to the chapel. There are often family and local traditions regarding the carrying of the coffin and if you have any doubts you should consult any family members or friends who may wish to be involved.

Choice of Music

Most cemetery and crematorium chapels have facilities for music to be played. They will be able to play cassette(s) or CD(s) that you supply and have organs which can be played either by someone provided by them, the funeral directors or yourself. A member of the family may wish to play. If you like, you can arrange for music to be played by a group of musicians. At a religious ceremony a choir from the deceased's church may wish to sing.

Many people, young and old, at some time express a wish as to what music they would like to be played at their funeral. Listening to music at home or at a concert someone may say, 'I'll have that played at my funeral'. Try to remember if the deceased has ever expressed such a wish. If not, the choice can be made by you or members of the family. Those attending the funeral, unless they have very definite views on the music to be played, will be happy to rely on the choice of the person arranging the funeral. If the deceased is a young person, perhaps the music could reflect that. Their friends might know what their favourite pieces were.

Where the service is held at a church or chapel the incumbent who will conduct the service will wish to discuss the choice of music. This will depend upon the facilities available. Music can usually be played when the mourners enter the church, and when they leave, and hymns will be sung during the service. Some hymns and psalms are traditionally sung at funerals and these may be suggested to you.

Music is a very personal matter and can have a very emotional effect on the whole proceedings. Funerals I have attended have been very different as far as the music is concerned. At one, the deceased had chosen her own music which included the hymn *All Things Bright and Beautiful* and a recording of Louis Armstrong singing *What a Wonderful World*. Another friend, despite being a person connected with the world of classical music, always said that she wanted Rod Stewart singing *I am Sailing* and, in addition to a selection of her favourite classical music chosen by her family, the last piece of music we heard as we left the crematorium was *I am Sailing*. One friend at her own request had a jazz band following her coffin to the cemetery. *Wotan's Farewell* and *Magic Fire Music* by Wagner was played at another cremation. An actor, showing a clear sense of humour, asked for *Smoke Gets in Your Eyes* to be played at his cremation.

If you make a specific choice you will probably be asked to supply a pre-recorded cassette or CD which can be played. The funeral directors will discuss this with you and will arrange for one of their attendants at the service to play the music in accordance with your instructions. It might be possible to rehearse the order of the service and the playing of the music. Funeral directors can help with the choice of music and may have some CDs/cassettes available from which you can make a selection.

If there is to be a cremation, the coffin will be placed on the plinth, called a catafalque, at the front of the chapel and will remain there during the service. Towards the end of the service, probably when the last piece of music is being played, either the coffin will be moved or the curtains will be closed. The funeral directors will then open the doors of the chapel so that the mourners can leave.

At all times during a service the funeral directors will indicate what is to be done and will be very supportive.

Accommodation for the Mourners

If any of those attending the funeral service have to travel from a distance, they will probably make their own travel arrangements but some may require overnight accommodation. People coming from abroad may need more than one night. If you have accommodation in your own home and wish to offer it, this would be a good solution. It would also ensure that you are not left alone after the funeral. You may, however, not have any room or prefer to be alone. Ask the person involved what kind of accommodation is required and then find the names and telephone numbers of local hotels or bed and breakfast places. You can give this information to the person concerned and then let him make his own arrangements. Although the question will probably not arise, be aware that if *you* make the arrangements then you are ultimately responsible for the cost.

Travel
Make certain that any mourners travelling from a distance know exactly where they are to meet and how to get there. They will need this information in order to give themselves sufficient time to get there. Give them specific local travel instructions.

Catering After the Funeral
If required, the funeral directors can deal with any catering arrangements or can recommend caterers who can deal with the matter.

The quantity and type of the food and drinks will, of course, be dependent upon how much money is available to spend. There could be sandwiches with tea and coffee for a small gathering. Hot snacks, canapés, and filled vol-au-vents, with mineral water, red and white wine could be provided. It is usually given as a buffet. There is really no limit. It is not usual to have a sit down meal after a funeral. A memorial dinner can be arranged for a later date if required.

It's quite common with small funerals for everyone who

comes to be invited back to the house where drinks and food are available. If this is to be done, you can prepare the food yourself with the assistance of a friend or a family member and leave it ready for the return after the funeral. Do not be too ambitious; fresh sandwiches and snacks are readily available at supermarkets and will not be too difficult to assemble. If you have left someone at the home of the deceased (as a useful security precaution against burglars, see page 75), he will be able to help prepare hot drinks such as tea or coffee if required.

Alternatively, you can arrange for local caterers to supply and prepare everything for you. They could do this on the premises while the funeral is taking place, which would also help with the problem of leaving the home empty.

If the gathering takes place at the home of the deceased, be prepared for some people who will want to stay longer than others. Devote as much time as people need, as it will be appreciated by them.

Some people like to gather at a neutral place such as a restaurant or a pub where all the arrangements can be made for food and drinks to be supplied. Restaurants, wine bars and public houses in the vicinity of the cemetery and crematorium may have a special service which they provide. I have been to gatherings in a conservatory attached to a public house, the annex of a wine bar, a private room in a restaurant, all within a short distance of the cemetery. Other venues have been a marquee in the person's garden, a church hall, and the upstairs room in a village pub. Similar arrangements can be made in the area near the home of the deceased.

If an outside venue is decided upon, agree with the caterer how long the gathering will last so that people can know when it is time to leave. When the allotted time is reached, try tactfully to let people know. Some who may not have met for a number of years may wish to go on somewhere else such as a wine bar or restaurant to continue talking together. In case they do, it would be kind to know the names of places nearby where they could go. Most people will make their own arrangements to travel home but keep the telephone number of a local taxi company available for those who wish to use it.

10

THE FUNERAL

Whatever the arrangements that have been made, ensure that all those who need to know are informed of the date, time and place of the funeral. If there is sufficient time, a short note giving that information can be sent by mail. An insertion can be made in local and national newspapers giving this information.

Give people enough time to get to the venue. Some people may have a long way to travel.

If the funeral is to leave from the home of the deceased, let the neighbours know the time that the hearse will be leaving. Where some of the family and friends have elected to accompany the hearse leaving from the home of the deceased, make arrangements for them to be comfortable in the house. Try to ensure that there is enough seating and that the bathroom and toilet are available for their use. If the weather is cold, arrange for some form of heating. When the weather is hot, keep the home as cool as possible by opening windows or providing a cooling fan. There should not be a very long wait for the funeral directors to arrive and most people will prefer to wear their outdoor coats while waiting. If there is going to be a long wait, offer to take their coats and have facilities ready to hang them up. A drinks tray might be a good idea or the offer of tea and coffee. This relieves the tension of waiting. Mostly people will talk in hushed voices or not talk at all but it is really not necessary. Encourage them, by your own example, to act as normally as possible.

Some people may never have been to a funeral before and be apprehensive. When they are all gathered and before the funeral director arrives, try to give them an idea of what will happen at the funeral and afterwards. Advise them who is required to travel with whom in the cars provided by the funeral directors. It is usual for the immediate family to travel alone in the first car behind the hearse. The following cars can carry more distant family members and friends. If some people are to travel in their own cars, obtain in advance from the funeral directors full travel instructions, so that they can follow easily, particularly if they do not live locally. Very often the crematorium or cemetery will be some distance from the home and the journey may take some time, possibly twenty minutes or half an hour; if they are separated from the cortège by traffic lights or difficult traffic conditions they need to be able to make their own way to the funeral. Answer as many questions as you are able to.

What to Wear

Most people think it is in good taste to wear dark clothing and men usually wear a black tie, but it is a matter of preference and these days black is not necessarily the dominant colour to wear. Some like to wear the clothes that the deceased had liked to see.

Some mourners, if the deceased belonged to an organisation which they represent, will wear uniforms, such as the Salvation Army, British Legion and the Red Cross. If the deceased was engaged in an occupation that required a uniform, the representatives from their employment may wear uniforms, such as the police, fire service, and the armed forces.

Floral Tributes

If floral tributes are to be given, some may come to the home of the deceased on the day of the funeral. These can be displayed outside or inside the home to await the arrival of the hearse. The funeral directors will collect the floral tributes and place them on the hearse or they can be carried out of the home by those who are giving them.

Leaving the Home

The funeral directors will send a chief funeral assistant, known as the conductor, to the home who will oversee all the arrangements. At the given time, he will advise those waiting that the hearse is present. He will invite all the mourners to go outside to get into the cars. Small travel packs of tissues could be on offer by the door as people go out. The pall bearers will accompany the hearse and as many of the funeral directors' assistants as are needed.

The conductor will collect any floral tributes and place them on the hearse if there is room or on the roof of the first and following cars. This will take a short time and the mourners if they require can watch or get into the cars to wait if they prefer.

The conductor will guide people into the cars and be very helpful throughout the proceedings. If anyone has any questions during this time, he will be happy to set his or her mind at rest.

Try to make sure that someone is left in the home during the time of the funeral: a neighbour, a friend or a family member who does not wish to attend the funeral. The fact that the home is to be left empty is quite likely to attract burglars. Even a dog would be a deterrent. If there is no one to help, make sure that all windows and doors are securely locked. You can explain to the conductor that you need to do this. If you think it worthwhile, inform the police beforehand that the home will be unoccupied and roughly for how long.

Neighbours and friends who are not attending the funeral service will probably wish to pay their respects and goodbyes and may gather outside the home to see the hearse leave. The hearse and following cars will move slowly through the immediate streets in a town or city and with the conductor walking in front of the hearse. Once out of the deceased's home environment the conductor will get into the hearse and it will proceed to the funeral venue. If the deceased was employed or belonged to a local club, the hearse can go past those premises in order for friends and colleagues to pay their respects.

At the Funeral
On arrival at the chapel in the cemetery or crematorium grounds, the hearse and cars will stop at the entrance if it has been arranged that the mourners will walk to the chapel behind the coffin. The pall bearers will be assembled by the funeral directors and the coffin will be carried to the chapel with the mourners following.

If the coffin is to be taken directly to the chapel, this will be done and the mourners will be assisted from the cars. When they are all gathered, either they will enter the chapel and sit down and then stand when the coffin is brought into the chapel and placed on the catafalque, or the coffin will be carried into the chapel with the mourners following, who will then sit. This can be discussed with the funeral directors at the time of arranging the funeral.

If a service is to be held at an ordinary church or chapel, the clergyman will advise on the details and will liaise with the funeral directors as to how the coffin is to be brought into the church.

If music has been agreed upon, it will be played when the coffin is brought into the chapel. The service will then take place, according to the arrangements that have been made. The chosen music will be played when the service is over.

When there is to be a cremation, the conductor will then invite everyone to leave the chapel and once outside will direct them to where the floral tributes have been placed so that they can be seen and the cards of condolence read. This gives the mourners time to compose themselves and to relax after an emotional occasion.

If there is to be a burial, the coffin will be carried out of the chapel and the conductor will invite the mourners to follow the coffin to the graveside. If a Church of England clergyman is present at the burial, he will read from the standard burial service and a short prayer may be said. Services which are conducted by a representative of a different religion will follow that religion's customs. If there is no religious representative present, usually a few words will be said by someone and the coffin will be lowered into the grave. Mourners can throw handfuls of earth or flowers onto the coffin before leaving the grave if they wish.

Different burial rituals may be followed in different areas, such as in parts of Scotland where relatives of the deceased may be given a decorative tape attached to the coffin which they hold and release as the coffin is lowered into the grave.

Unless expressly requested, floral tributes are not interred with the coffin. The floral tributes will be placed beside the grave. The conductor will then lead the way back to the waiting cars. The mourners can then be taken to the venue where the reception is to take place.

Gratuities
There is no accepted ruling regarding tipping the attending staff of the funeral directors but some families like to do this, particularly if they have received kind and sensitive

attention. The money can be given discreetly to the conductor at the funeral or can be left at the office of the funeral directors for distribution a few days later. Tips are not generally expected by the staff, but they are appreciated.

Gratuities can also be given to the cemetery staff associated with the burial and crematorium staff if wished. A sum could be left with the cemetery or crematorium manager for distribution.

If it is decided to give gratuities, ask a member of the family or a close friend to be responsible for this. It should be someone who can behave discreetly. Give him the money before leaving for the funeral so that you do not have to worry about this item.

If the funeral director's representative and staff are known personally to the family or the person organising the funeral, they could be offered some refreshments and invited to the gathering after the funeral. This might happen when the funeral directors have conducted other funerals for the family or knew the deceased or in a rural area where this is customary. If the invitation is accepted, they normally stay only a short time. If gratuities are to be given, they could be given at that time.

After the Funeral
After the funeral comes the time for talking and remembering. If the gathering is to take place in the home of the deceased, give people time to relax before bringing in the food. You might like to offer alcoholic drinks which could help.

It will not be long before people are talking to each other, remembering the deceased and reminiscing about old times and mutual acquaintances. If people from different environments do not know each other, such as colleagues from work, relatives, church and club members, introduce them to each other. They will probably have remembrances to tell. It may have been a while – possibly years – since some people or family members have met; this will be an occasion for them to renew old acquaintances.

Some people will wish to remain talking for quite a time, others will leave early. If the gathering is at the home of the deceased there is really no time limit expected for those who will be left. Once one person decides to leave, others will probably follow. If you wish the gathering to end by a certain time, do not be afraid to tell people. When the gathering is at an outside venue, people will be aware that there is probably a time when it will finish.

It is not really the responsibility of the funeral organiser, but it is helpful if everybody has a method of getting home. It will also help you to know how and when people will be leaving. If alcoholic drinks have been served, driving home may not be advisable so taxis may be required. Some people will have made arrangements to be collected or will need to make a phone call. Where there is no telephone on the property a mobile phone would be useful. A restaurant or pub will probably have a local taxi firm they deal with and will usually telephone for taxis if required.

At a funeral I went to, there were people attending from different times in the life of the deceased: some from when she was a child, some from her early work days, her family days and other friends and family. Many did not know each other which could have made the situation difficult. The family solved this by filling a very large picture frame with a collage of photographs of the deceased from her childhood to the present time which was placed on an easel for all to see. This proved a great talking point as many of the people present were also shown in the photographs and any awkwardness was immediately dispelled. This method also got people talking to each other and formal introductions were kept to a minimum.

A 'get together' was arranged after the funeral of my aunt at the sheltered accommodation where she lived. Most of the elderly residents were unable to attend the funeral. The warden, knowing what the residents liked, kindly agreed to arrange a tea for the residents in the communal hall. The family returned to the hall after the funeral and talked to all her friends and neighbours and, as much as can be said about these occasions, everyone enjoyed themselves, talking about 'Lila' and the good times they had all had together.

"SMITH Jenny. The family of the late Jenny Smith would like to thank all who sent kind messages of sympathy following the death of Jenny."

"SMITH. Henry Smith would like to express his sincere thanks to all relatives and friends for their kind messages of sympathy and flowers received following the death of his dear wife Jenny. Thanks to everyone who attended the funeral service. He would also like to express his thanks to the staff of the Hospice for their care and kindness during Jenny's illness. Thanks are also due to the Rev. Bill Jones for the comforting church service."

"SMITH. The family of Jenny Smith wish to thank all relatives, friends and neighbours for their kindness, support messages of sympathy, cards and donations to the RNLI, which have been a great comfort after their recent bereavement. Thanks to Father Brian O'Connor for the Requiem Mass and to everyone for attending."

Fig. 5. Newspaper entries of thanks for sympathy.

Saying Thank You

After the funeral, cards and letters of condolence and floral tributes should be acknowledged. This could be done by writing separate notes of thanks to individual people or by inserting an entry in the local newspaper (see Fig. 5) or both.

11

DEALING WITH PROPERTY

Seeking Legal Advice
Sorting out a personal estate, obtaining Probate if necessary, and making sure that everything is paid over to the final beneficiaries is a much more complicated matter than you might expect. It is full of pitfalls and problems for anyone who is unfamiliar with the procedures.

For this reason, I would suggest that you need to seek legal advice if matters are at all complicated.

The sort of estate that you can sort out for yourself without necessarily including any legal help might have the following features:

1.   It might be below the threshold (see Appendix III) so that an actual Grant of Probate is not required.
2.   If above the threshold, it could be very simple in that it is still well below the threshold for Inheritance Tax, property is not involved, there is no link with a trust fund from a previous death, and all the beneficiaries are easily ascertainable.

In cases such as this, I would suggest that you might be able to go ahead by yourself, but keep in mind the possibility of needing legal advice to resolve any unexpected problems.

I strongly recommend that you seek advice from a solicitor if the deceased's estate contains one or more of the following features:

(a) A substantial estate approaching or exceeding the threshold for Inheritance Tax (see Appendix III).
(b) Ownership of property, or valuable paintings, antiques, jewellery or collections.
(c) Involvement with trust funds within the family.
(d) Any problem of not being able to find beneficiaries, or there being disputes between beneficiaries.
(e) Any business assets including shares in private companies.
(f) Anything else of a legal kind that you feel you are not sure about.

Property and Land

If the deceased owned property or land in England or Wales, it is necessary to find the deeds relating to that property. If the deceased had a mortgage on the property, the deeds will be held by the lender (a building society, finance company, bank, or possibly a private lender). If there was no mortgage, the deeds may be held on behalf of the deceased by a bank or a solicitor. They may be in a deposit box in a bank or a deeds repository. They may have been kept by the deceased amongst his private papers.

Joint Ownership of Property

If the property was jointly owned by the deceased and another person as *joint tenants*, then the property will automatically pass to the surviving joint owner. The survivor should send a copy of the death certificate to the Land Registry and the name of the deceased will be removed from the register. If the property was jointly owned by the deceased and another person as *tenants in common*, the share of the property owned by the deceased will become part of the estate and can be dealt with accordingly.

Is the Property Registered?

Most properties are now registered at the Land Registry (see Appendix II). The first time a property is registered (which is usually at the time of a sale or transfer), all the existing deeds and documents have to be sent to the Registry. Once land is registered, the original old documents are destroyed by the Land Registry.

In order to find out if the property is registered, you can ask for a search of the Land Registry Index Map, using form 96 which you can obtain from the Registry. There is no fee for this service.

If you wish to make a search in the name of the deceased to find out what property is registered in his name, you should use form 104 but this cannot be done until you have obtained a Grant of Probate or Letters of Administration.

If the property has been registered, a Land Certificate (or a Charge Certificate where the property is mortgaged) will have been issued. The certificate shows who owns the land and who has a mortgage, which may be more than one company. The Land Registry keep a record of where they last sent the certificates. They may therefore be able to help you locate where the documents are held.

You can apply for copies of the entries in the Register. Obtain form 109 from the Land Registry and return it to them completed with the information requested and a remittance to pay for the copies.

Forms 104 and 109 can also be obtained from any branch of The Stationery Office or a law stationer's. The Land Registry issue a number of leaflets relating to dealing with property which may be helpful to you.

Unregistered Land or Property

If the property is not registered, there is no central record of property ownership that you can check. It is only necessary to provide deeds going back 30 years from the present day in order to prove ownership, but the deeds relating to the deceased's property may be numerous and cover many years, showing all the previous owners and how the property was transferred from one to another. The deeds will consist of conveyances, indentures, plans and maps, and the final document should show the transfer to the deceased. In the case of unregistered land, some of the deeds may be very old and handwritten. These deeds may have been held by the deceased at home. If not, try asking at the bank or solicitor of the deceased, if he had one.

It will be necessary to register any unregistered land or property. If the deeds are not readily available and you do not know where they are, it can be very difficult. You will need to seek the professional advice of a solicitor.

Mortgage

If there is a mortgage on the property, there may be a mortgage protection policy in existence which will pay the balance owing on the death of the owner. The mortgage company will probably know about this. When available, a sealed copy of the Grant of Probate should be forwarded to the insurers who will either pay the proceeds directly to the mortgage holders or pay the money to the executors who can then repay the mortgage.

If there is no policy, the mortgage will be repaid when the property is sold. A sealed copy of the Grant of Probate should be sent to the mortgage holders advising them whether the property is to be sold or transferred to beneficiaries named in the will. In the latter case, the mortgage holders will give advice on how the matter should be dealt with.

Sale of Property

If the property is to be sold, it will be necessary to seek the services of a solicitor since only a solicitor or a company specialising in conveyancing is able to draw up the required documents. The executors are duty bound to sell the property for the best possible market price so that the money from the sale can be added to the residue of the estate for distribution.

The property can be put into the hands of an estate agent who will deal with the sale. An estate agent will charge a percentage of the sale price, plus expenses, and the amounts should be agreed when instructions for the sale are given. The sale could be advertised or negotiated but cannot be completed until the Grant of Probate has been received and there is clearance from the Inland Revenue Capital Taxes Office (see Chapter 13, page 110).

After the Grant of Probate

If any registered property was owned by the deceased without a mortgage, a sealed copy of the Grant of Probate should be sent to the Land Registry with a request that the property be transferred into the name of the executors as the new owners. The new owners will then be sent a Land Certificate and be in a position to sell the property. If the property has been bequeathed to someone in the will, a copy of the will should also be sent to the Land Registry. The land will then be transferred into the name of the new owner and a Land Certificate sent.

If the land is unregistered, the deeds, together with a copy of the will (if there is one) and a sealed copy of the Grant of Probate should be sent to the Land Registry who will then register the land and issue a Land Certificate in the name of the new owner. Send by Special Delivery.

12

SORTING OUT HOUSEHOLD
AND PERSONAL ITEMS

Now that the formalities have been completed and the
funeral is over, you will hopefully have time at your leisure
to deal with the personal, household and other belongings
of the deceased.

A good supply of large plastic rubbish bags will be very
useful at this time as you will inevitably come across many
things that, reluctant though you may be, will have to be
thrown away.

Pets and Animals
If any pets are being looked after by other people or have
been left in the care of an animal sanctuary or charity, a
final decision has to be made regarding their welfare. If
you are unable to find them a permanent new home, the
animal sanctuary should be advised and asked to look after
them and find them a new home. If the animal has been at
a cattery or kennel, it can be collected by its new owner or
an animal charity. Any outstanding fees due to a cattery or
kennel will have to be paid and entered as a sum to be
deducted on the Probate application.

Jewellery

Whatever happens to the jewellery, whether it is specifically bequeathed, sold, or forms part of the residue of the estate, it will have to be valued for Probate. The value for Probate of any items of value to be sold should be the expected sale price. This is not the same as the insurance value which could be higher.

Jewellery which has been bequeathed to certain friends or relatives of the deceased can now be distributed provided it doesn't need to be sold to meet debts. The remaining jewellery, however, forms part of the general estate, goes to the final beneficiaries of the will and cannot be sold or disposed of until Probate has been obtained.

If it has to be sold, a good jeweller can give a valuation. He will make a charge for this service based on the total value of the jewellery. Jewellery can be sold to a dealer in secondhand jewellery, by auction, privately or by advertising it for sale in a local newspaper, specialist magazine if it is antique jewellery, or on the Internet.

Vehicles

Any vehicles (car, van, motorcycle or scooter) owned by the deceased, if not specifically bequeathed, may have to be sold once the Grant of Probate has been obtained. For this, you will need the documents relating to the vehicles including the vehicle registration book and MOT test certificate (if applicable).

First, though, you need to ascertain whether the vehicles were wholly owned by the deceased or whether they were purchased with a loan and, if so, how much of the loan is still outstanding and needs to be paid, and how this is to be organised.

Passport
If the deceased had a passport this should be sent to the Passport Office (see Appendix II), together with a certified copy of the death certificate.

Driving Licence
Return the deceased's driving licence to the DVLA (see Appendix II).

Library Books
If the deceased belonged to a public library and left some books in the home, inform the library of the death and return the books and any library tickets. The library will probably not require to see a copy of the death certificate, but it might be helpful to take one with you to the library in case they do ask to see it.

Book Clubs and Music Clubs
If there is any evidence amongst the deceased's papers that he belonged to a book or music club where he received items through the mail, the clubs should be advised of the death and asked to cancel the subscription. It is sometimes difficult to speak to these clubs on the telephone so give notice of the death in writing, quoting the account number if you have found it.

Personal and Household Goods
Start by putting things, such as partly used cleaning material, cosmetics, old unwanted magazines, bathroom toiletries and anything else that cannot be passed on for use, into the plastic bags.

If the deceased left a will giving instructions as to the disposal of his personal and household goods, there may be bequests of certain items to specific people. Now is the time to arrange for those bequests to be given to the people concerned. Get in touch with them and ask them how they would like to receive the bequest. If it is a small item they may ask for it to be sent by mail or they may wish to call to collect it. If any cost is involved in dealing with a bequest, this can be shown as a debt to the estate.

Where household goods are part of the residue of the estate and have been bequeathed to one person or several persons, then they have the choice of what to do with them. Usually, if they are bequeathed jointly they will have to be sold and the value added to the residue of the estate for distribution. They may decide to keep mementoes and to give the rest away. Charities such as Save the Children, Oxfam, Help the Aged and various hospices have shops where second hand goods are sold. If there is a large amount of furniture, etc, charities may be prepared to make arrangements to collect.

Where there are no specific bequests, then household goods such as furniture, kitchen equipment, linen, china, electrical appliances, etc, can be sold and the proceeds added to the estate. It is not easy to sell ordinary second hand furniture and household objects but you could advertise suitable items in the local newspapers. Estimates of the amounts to be obtained will have to be shown in the Probate application, and the notes which accompany the form are a useful guide.

Photographs

Many people take photographs to remind them of holidays, special occasions, friends and family. You are very possibly going to find photograph albums and loose photographs amongst the deceased's possessions. These will form part of the residue of the estate but if there is no will, they could be offered to the next of kin or to the people in the photographs if you know who they are. If they become your property, you might like to make up an album of those you wish to keep before disposing of the others. If photographs are to be kept, it is a good idea to write on the back of the photograph the names of the subjects and also, if known, the date when the photographs were taken.

Family Bible
A family Bible may be in the possession of the deceased. This might contain handwritten entries relating to births, deaths and marriages of members of the family. Ideally it should be passed to the next of kin or to someone in the family who is tracing the family history. The person who is to receive the residue of the estate may decide to keep the Bible or offer it to someone else in the family. If it has been a tradition to keep records in a family Bible, a member of the family may wish to continue the custom.

Family History
The deceased may have been tracing his family history and have a family tree and numerous documents which could be of interest to another member of the family. There may be correspondence showing that someone else is also preparing a family history and the deceased's work could be passed on to him or her. Provided there is no family member interested in working on a family history, if it is well documented it could be passed to the Society of Genealogists who are pleased to receive family histories for their archives.

The Internet
When you are seeking information on any subject and you have access to the Internet, look for information there. Given the time, you can discover information on almost any subject. You will be able to find out where you can dispose of any items of furniture and get some idea of their worth. This may eventually save you time and will give you an idea of where to ask for further assistance.

Antiques, Books and Pictures
If you think there are any antiques or original paintings amongst the household goods, then it is necessary to obtain a proper valuation so that, if they are to be sold, they can be sold at the best possible price. Look for the names of reputable antique dealers in the telephone directory and make an appointment for their representatives to call to value the items. Dealers may make a charge for this valuation, based upon the value of the items involved. They may make an offer to purchase the items in question or they may be able to suggest the best way to sell them. If you are doubtful about their advice, consult more than one dealer. Dealers' valuations may vary considerably. It might be worthwhile to purchase a specialist magazine or seek advice from your local or a national museum specialising in the items concerned. Anything really unusual or valuable could be sent for auction. Any estimated amounts will have to be shown on the Probate application.

Collections and Memorabilia
If the deceased had a special collection that was accumulated over the years, it could be offered for sale in a magazine specialising in that subject, or offered in the local or a national newspaper. However, before doing that, it is essential to obtain a true valuation. Many collections, such as a stamp collection, war memorabilia, posters, glass, porcelain, figurines, teaspoons, theatre programmes, dolls, comic albums, coins, etc, could have a great deal of value. It is surprising to some of us and difficult to appreciate the sort of things people collect as a hobby over many years. They may have no intrinsic value to anyone else but they certainly meant something to the deceased and it seems sad that they will have to be disposed of. You may consider that the collection has very little value, but give it the benefit of an expert valuation. There are museums specialising in

most things. There is a *Directory of Museums* which should be available in your local library and a telephone call to the museum in question should be able to answer your questions. An enquiry posted on the Internet might also be a way of gaining some information about the collection.

General Clearance

A local company can be asked to clear the premises of all goods. Such companies often advertise in local newspapers. They usually make no charge and pay for the items that they take. If you find it difficult to dispose of the household goods, tell them that they must take everything, not just those things that they find of commercial value. However, most of these companies offer very little recompense. I recall many years ago when my mother died I had to clear her rented accommodation very quickly and employed a local company, since I was unable, at that time, to take any furniture or household goods myself. I gave them the keys and was not present when they called but I found it very upsetting when I returned to find that they had indeed taken everything. They had ripped up carpets, taken down the curtains and curtain rails, and left cupboards open and empty. At that time they offered fifty pounds for the total contents of the flat.

If you have to dispose of furniture and household goods in this way, make sure that all personal correspondence, statements and accounts, credit cards and anything required for Probate and estate records are removed and safely stored before giving instructions for disposal.

Where it is essential to clear rented property swiftly, it is sometimes distressing to have to dispose of the belongings of the deceased in this fashion. It does seem sad that the lifetime possessions of one person have to be disposed of in this way, but there may be no choice.

Another alternative is to put everything into boxes and

send it with the unwanted furniture and all other items to a local auction house. It is surprising what people will buy at auctions, particularly dealers, and you may be pleased at the total amount realised by the sale. There will be a buyer's and a seller's premium to pay, but this may be the easiest and quickest way of dealing with everything.

It is virtually impossible to sell secondhand clothes unless they are expensive designer clothes or good quality collectors' items. Clothes that are clean and wearable can be given to the charity shops but even they will not take all types of secondhand clothing and you may have to dispose of much of it by throwing it away in plastic bags however distasteful and wasteful this may be.

Some local councils will collect all the unwanted items by appointment and dispose of them. Our local council will collect unwanted furniture and household items which they use to give to homeless families when they are rehoused.

13

GETTING PROBATE

Executors
If the deceased has left a will naming an executor or two or more executors, in the first instance anyone named as an executor does not have to accept the responsibility if he does not wish to do so. However, the person making a will usually asks someone to be an executor before naming him in the will so that the question of someone refusing to act as an executor does not often arise. Where there is more than one named executor, some may choose to act and some may retire in favour of leaving a smaller number or even only one person to act as sole executor.

If a named sole executor does not wish to proceed as executor, he can renounce it. Then, the person named in the will as the beneficiary of the residue of the estate after all bequests have been made has first priority to take over. Legal advice is then needed.

Wills do not usually state that an executor should receive a fee unless he is acting in a professional capacity. An executor will receive legitimate expenses from the estate and is sometimes a beneficiary. If a solicitor or bank is appointed as executor, the solicitor or bank will charge their usual fees for dealing with the matter.

Wills sometimes provide that if a beneficiary has died

before the deceased, then the beneficiary's children or someone else should inherit. If there is no such provision, then the amount of the legacy falls into the residue of the estate.

Letters of Administration

These are applied for where a person has died intestate, which means that he left no will. Also there is a procedure called Letters of Administration with Will Annexed; these are applied for when there is no executor named in the will, or if the executor declines to act. There is a specific priority of order as to who may apply for Letters of Administration, i.e. take over the executorship, and again as to who should inherit in the case of intestacy with specific rules regarding children. Legal advice is needed.

   Letters of Administration are granted by the Probate Office in the place of a Grant of Probate and are used in order to administer the estate. The next of kin applies to the Probate Office in the same way as applying for a Grant of Probate; instead of the issue of a Grant of Probate bearing a court seal attached to a copy of the will, Letters of Administration with a court seal are issued. If there is a valid will with no named executor, Letters of Administration are granted according to the same priority of order (usually the residuary legatee first) and a copy of the will is attached to the Letters of Administration. A solicitor may be needed to deal with the arrangements.

Probate

Do you need Probate?

If there is no property and the total estate (including bank accounts, insurance policies, investments, etc) does not exceed the threshold (see Appendix III), it is not necessary to apply for Probate. Application can be made directly to the various holders so that the money can be released for distribution, according to the will, to the beneficiaries. The executor sends a copy of the will and a certified death certificate, together with the relevant documents, such as an insurance policy and bank statements, to the holders. Although not strictly necessary, some banks, building societies and insurance companies will still ask to see a sealed copy of the Grant of Probate even if the amount is small. Others will release the money on sight of the death certificate. When sending original documents by mail it is advisable to send them by recorded or special delivery and to keep a copy of each document sent.

Where property has been left by the deceased, a sealed copy of the Grant of Probate will be required in order to sell or deal with that property.

Sometimes third party or industrial insurance may have been taken out on the life of the deceased: a son could have insured a parent, a parent could have insured a child, an employer could have insured an employee. In these cases, payment is made directly to the person who took out the policy and the payment does not have to be included in the Probate application. Claims on this type of insurance can be settled without a Grant of Probate or Letters of Administration since they do not form part of the estate.

If the total value of the estate is above the threshold, it will be necessary to apply for Probate before any of the money or assets can be released.

Who Should Apply for Probate?

The executors of the will should apply for Probate and may need help from a solicitor. A Grant of Probate cannot be made to anyone under the age of eighteen years.

Where to Obtain Probate Forms

You can obtain all the necessary Probate application forms and information by telephoning the Principal Probate

Office in London (see Appendix II). There is an answer-phone; leave your name and address, and a set of forms will be sent to you by mail. Alternatively, ring your local District Registry or Sub-Registry (see your local phone book). If you prefer, you can apply in person to the Probate Office where you can obtain the forms.

You should carefully read all the literature and information that is sent to you by the Probate Office before you attempt to complete the forms. Guidance note IHT 206 is issued by the Inland Revenue and Guide PA2 by the Probate Office. These will be sent to you together with the application forms. They are very helpful and are issued for people wishing to make a personal application for a Grant of Probate without using a solicitor. There are a number of forms which will need to be completed. These are:

Form PA1   Application form.
Form PA5   Matrimonial Home Information.
For estates well below the Inheritance Tax threshold,
    form IHT 205.
For larger estates where IHT will have to be paid, you
    will need form IHT 200, with various accompanying
    sub-sections, and you will need a solicitor's help too.

Once the approximate value of the estate is ascertained, contact the Capital Taxes Office in Nottingham (see Appendix II) to find out whether an Inland Revenue Account form needs to be completed, and if so, which one.

When you have read the literature you may find that it is not necessary to complete all the forms that have been sent to you. Form PA1, the application form, is the form which must be completed by all applicants. If you find it too difficult you can seek the advice of the local Citizens Advice Bureau or a local Community Law Office. You may wish at this stage to decide to request the assistance of a solicitor, bearing in mind that the solicitor will charge a fee.

Once you have completed the forms you will need to send them to the Probate Registry where you wish to be interviewed (see page 107) or to the Probate Registry which controls the local office where you wish to be interviewed.

It takes time and effort to gather the assets in order to complete the Probate forms. The forms required are the Probate Application Form, and the Account of the Estate Forms which require a full account of the estate. You will need to know the total value of the assets of the estate and the total amount of outstanding debts. Even if it is a small estate, you can expect it to take about three to six months before Probate is granted. It takes a considerable amount of time, involving correspondence and telephone calls, to obtain details of all the financial arrangements of the deceased. If it is a large estate with property involved, it can take a year, eighteen months or several years to obtain a Grant of Probate.

Gathering the Information – Assets
First send a certified copy death certificate to each of the holders of assets such as banks, building societies, insurance companies, Premium Bonds Office, National Savings Office, registrars of companies in which shares are held, etc, together with details such as the full name and address of the deceased, account numbers, certificate numbers and policy numbers of the documents that you have. Advise them of the death and ask for details of the amounts in the accounts available to the estate as at the date of death and/or the number of shares registered.

Shares
If the shares are held in a company quoted on the Stock Market, information as to the value of the shares held can be obtained from the quoted prices in the national newspapers.

The Times, The Daily Telegraph, The Financial Times and other national newspapers publish many share prices every day, including all the largest companies. The quoted share prices can also be obtained from the Internet and from the text pages on the television. However, the value you need is the quoted value of the shares at the date of death. The *Stock Exchange Daily Official List* for the date of death can be obtained from the FT Information Services (see Appendix II). These prices are quoted per share and will have to be multiplied by the number of shares held in order to reach a total value. If an exact valuation is required, you need legal or financial help to apply the "quarter up" rule.

The value of any shares held in private companies not quoted on the Stock Exchange should be obtained from the companies themselves by writing to the Company Secretary who should be able to tell you how you can obtain a valuation of the company shares.

Unit Trusts

Holdings in Unit Trusts can be treated in the same way as those in straightforward shares. A letter to the Unit Trust managers named on the certificates should request details of the value of the holding as at the date of death.

Insurance Policies

It may be that there are some insurance policies amongst the effects of the deceased where you are unable to trace the present address of the insurance company, particularly if the deceased was elderly and had held the policies since early life; the companies may have changed their name by merging with others or moved their head offices. A publication called the *Insurance Directory* gives addresses and telephone numbers of all existing insurance companies and those that have merged with them. The directory may be available at your local reference library, or you could ask any local insurance company that you deal with whether they have a copy.

When you give the company the name of the deceased and the number of the policy, they will most certainly be able to tell you if the policy has a value and will give you instructions as to how to make a claim.

Banks

If you are near to the banks in question, a visit there with all the documents, such as recent statements, paying in books, current cheque books and a certified death certificate, would save a great deal of correspondence. Banks often have 'personal advisors' available to assist people with queries without the necessity of making an appointment. Bank assistants will be able to give you all the information you need. They will take a copy of the death certificate and return the original to you. They will be able to advise you of the accounts held by the deceased, current or deposit, and the value of them. They will also advise of any existing direct debits, standing orders and any loan accounts with sums due to the bank. Ask for written confirmation of the amounts held in each account.

At the same time, you can ask whether the bank is holding any deeds or documents on behalf of the deceased and whether the deceased held a safety deposit box with the bank.

Missing Bank Accounts

If you think that there may be bank accounts that you are unable to find, the National Association of Bank Customers (see Appendix II) can help you to search for and locate those accounts. You should send them the full name and address of the deceased (including his previous address if he had only lived at the last address for a short time). Information about the bank accounts that you do know about should also be given.

Building Societies

A visit to the local branch of a building society can also save a great deal of correspondence. Take the death certificate, together with any payment or account books or recent statements, to the local branch of the society and they will give you all the information you need. They will take a copy of the death certificate and return the original to you. Ask the society to give you written confirmation of the amounts available in any accounts. If you think there may be other accounts with that society that you have not located, ask them to make a search of all their records to find whether the deceased held any other accounts.

National Savings

National Savings accounts, bonds and saving certificates are dealt with by the National Savings (see Appendix II). Form DNS 904 can be obtained from any Post Office, together with free addressed envelopes. Send the completed form together with details of the accounts, certificates and bonds held in the name of the deceased, together with a certified copy of the death certificate and ask for details of the amounts available.

Premium Bonds and National Lottery Tickets

Premium Bonds are dealt with by a different office of the National Savings (see Appendix II). If you think that the deceased may have held Premium Bonds and you can find no documents, ask for a search to be made. Premium Bonds cannot be transferred into the name of any other person. They can be held by the estate for 12 months after the death of a holder (when there is always a chance that they might win!) but must then be repaid.

National Lottery tickets remain valid for the dates for which they are issued. If the deceased held any winning lottery tickets, they become part of the estate of the deceased and must be included in the assets shown on the Probate forms. A claim against a lottery ticket must be made within 180 days of the date of the win.

Bond or lottery prizes won after the date of death are after the event and do not form part of the estate, so the asset value of a premium bond is the face value at the date of death.

Bookmakers

If the deceased had a credit account with a bookmaker there may be evidence such as statements and receipts of that amongst his papers. There are no enforceable laws governing betting and each bookmaker will apply his own rules. Bookmakers' accounts are usually settled monthly. If there are monies due to the bookmakers they may request payment or if there is money due to the deceased they may choose to settle the account. If the deceased had ongoing future bets, such as on the result of the forthcoming Derby or Grand National, or indeed of any bet, the bookmaker may allow that bet to stand, or may decide to cancel all bets. Negotiations will have to be conducted with the bookmaker. If the bookmaker does settle an account in favour of the deceased this amount must be included in the Probate application.

Property

If the deceased owned any property the full market value of that property has to be given on the Probate application form. A professional valuation is not required, but an accurate estimate of the amount for which the property could be sold. The District Valuer who is an employee of the Inland Revenue will check the estimated value of the property. If you have no idea at all of the value of the property you could look in the windows of a local estate agent to compare the prices of nearby similar properties for sale or request an estate agent to visit the property to give a valuation. Estate agents will give a valuation free of charge if they are to be instructed to deal with the sale at some time. Advise the estate agent that you are seeking a valuation for Probate purposes as this may affect his valuation.

If there was a mortgage on the property, its details should be entered on the Probate forms.

Vehicles

Any vehicles, cars, vans, motorcycles, scooters, etc, that belonged to the deceased will have to be valued and an estimated value based on a selling price included in the Probate application. If the deceased had purchased the vehicles with the assistance of a loan, the amount owing on the loan should be shown in the sums to be deducted on the Probate application unless there was an insurance policy which paid on the death. Check the agreement to see whether life cover was included. Most vehicles have a quoted secondhand trade price and this can be obtained from a car dealer or one of the car price guides available at newsagents. This would only apply if the vehicle is in very good second-hand condition and a lower price may be offered when it comes to a sale. A fair estimate should be shown in the Probate application.

Other Goods

An estimate of the value of jewellery, household goods, paintings, collections and other belongings of the deceased is also required for Probate purposes. A professional valuation is not required, but if you have any doubts and cannot give an estimated value, then a professional valuation should be obtained. All that is needed is an estimate of the amount for which they could be sold. The value of household goods and clothes should be included but as they will mostly be unsaleable, a nominal sum for these items should be shown on the Probate forms.

Employment
If the deceased was employed, any money due from his employers must be shown. This should include accrued holiday entitlement, pensions and savings held for the deceased by employers. A full written statement of what is due to the deceased should be obtained from the employers and included in the Probate forms.

Gathering the Information – Debts
Write to any people or organisations who you think have a claim on the estate of the deceased. Send them a certified copy of the death certificate and ask for evidence of how much the deceased owed at the date of death. Money may be owed in respect of rent, Visa, Mastercard, American Express and other credit cards, store credit cards, catalogue credit purchases, television and video rentals, Council Tax, Income Tax, water rates, mortgage, electricity, gas, telephone, newspaper and milk deliveries. There may be other weekly, monthly or yearly payments that are due but most of them will have ceased as at the date of death and will be calculated to that date.

It will be necessary to obtain written statements, calculated to the date of death, from anyone to whom money was owed at the date of death. These amounts will need to be included in the Probate application and will be deducted from the assets on the final total in the Grant of Probate.

Some credit card companies and others arrange insurance to cover debts left on a person's death. Ask the companies the deceased dealt with whether such insurance existed for him. If so, the debts won't need to be included in the Probate forms.

Newspaper Enquiry

If you are in any doubt and you feel that there may be money due to or from the deceased that you have been unable to locate, or you feel that there may be someone somewhere who has an interest in the estate, you could advertise for creditors by inserting an advertisement in a local and national newspaper asking them to contact you.

There is also a special arrangement with the *London Gazette* for advertising for creditors. The information to be published has to give the name of the deceased, the date of death and the name and address of the person to whom claims should be made. It is advisable to give a time limit for claims to be received; usually this is two months. The *London Gazette* will only accept advertisements from private advertisers after Probate has been obtained. Most newspapers will accept advertisements at any time. If you do advertise, you should use a box number as you may receive false information and you do not want anyone contacting you personally until you have decided that their claim is genuine. If you are using the services of a solicitor, you should discuss this aspect of the estate and he will arrange for an advertisement if he thinks it necessary.

Probate with a Will

Once you have gathered all the information necessary and completed the forms, send them to the Probate Office together with the certified death certificate and the original will. It is also a good idea to send photocopies of the statements and letters you have received stating the monies due to the deceased and the debts to be paid, together with the funeral account. The invoice showing the funeral costs should be included as a debt. If possible, keep copies of documents and send the originals by recorded or special delivery. If you are near the Probate Office you can deliver the forms by hand but ask for a receipt. Send all correspondence to the Probate Registry where you wish to be interviewed, or which controls the local office where you wish to be interviewed. Do not send to the local office itself.

Probate Interview
Unless a solicitor is applying for the probate it will be necessary in due course for you to attend at the Probate Office for an interview before the Grant of Probate can be issued. Section 1 of the application form refers to the proposed interview and asks you to state where you would like the interview to take place. There are a number of venues available and a leaflet is sent to you with the application form showing the addresses of them. The Principal Probate Office in London is open every weekday, but some of the local offices have more restricted openings.

It may take some time before you are called for an interview. If you can be available at short notice, then the interview may take place more quickly. You will be asked on the application form whether you can attend an interview at short notice. This is not an intimidating interview. It will take place in a small private room at the Probate Office. The interviewing officer will go through the papers and will answer any questions you may have. The interview usually takes about 20 minutes.

At the interview you will be asked to confirm that all the written information you have given on the forms is correct and that there have been no changes since you completed the forms. You may find it helpful to take with you to that interview all the original documents on which the information you have given is based. You will be asked to swear a simple oath to the effect that the information remains the same. If you prefer, you may affirm instead of swearing an oath. The interviewing officer is a Commissioner for Oaths and is empowered to administer an oath or affirmation.

At the interview the interviewing officer will give you some idea of how long it will be before you receive the Grant of Probate. A straightforward Grant of Probate should be available within a month from the interview. You will be asked how many copies of the Grant of Probate you require. These will be official copies with a Registry seal and will be acceptable to the authorities and institutions who ask for copies of the Grant of Probate. Photocopies of the Grant of Probate without the official seal would not be acceptable. If you have a number of claims to make, it is helpful to have several sealed copies of the Grant of Probate as it will save time waiting for the official copies to be returned to you by different institutions in turn.

Probate Fee

Application for a Grant of Probate requires a fee to be paid. The fee is payable at the interview not when the initial application is made. The Grant of Probate will not be issued until the fee is paid. The Probate Office will tell you the amount of the fee when arranging the interview. See Appendix III. There is no fee if the estate falls below the threshold for Probate. A small charge is also made for each extra sealed copy of the Grant of Probate that is requested.

Inheritance Tax

All estates are subject to tax but in most cases no tax will be payable since an allowance is made before tax has to be paid. No tax is payable, however high the value of the estate, on whatever part of the estate is left to the surviving spouse. The threshold at which tax becomes payable is shown on the application form. This usually rises each year in line with inflation. See Appendix III for the current threshold. It is a considerable sum, but if the deceased owned property and had jewellery, savings accounts, shares in companies, a car and substantial insurances, the value of the estate can easily exceed it.

Tax is currently levied at a standard rate of 40% on any amount in the estate above the threshold. Unlike other forms of tax there is no lower or higher rate and the full 40% is payable . If tax is payable, this has to be paid before the Grant of Probate is issued. If you are unable personally to pay the amount required by the Inland Revenue, a dilemma may arise. Although there is sufficient money in the estate to pay the Inheritance Tax, the money cannot be obtained until the tax has been paid! In that case you need to make special arrangements.

If there is some money in a National Savings Bank Account, Premium Bonds or National Savings Certificates it can be used to pay the Inheritance Tax. Advise the Probate Office that this money will be needed to pay the Inheritance Tax and the Probate office will provide a special letter. This letter together with the account book, certificates or other documents should be sent to the National Savings Office. The National Savings Office will then send a cheque for the tax directly to the Probate Office. Any balance left can be applied for in the normal manner after a Grant of Probate has been issued.

Another way in which money from the estate can be obtained to pay the Inheritance Tax is from a building society. It is possible that upon request the society will release the amount of money required by sending a cheque directly to the Probate Office.

If the deceased had a bank account, that bank may agree to lend the executors the amount required to pay the Inheritance Tax. They will do this if the documents show that there are sufficient assets in the estate to cover the loan. The bank will, of course, charge interest on the loan which will have to be paid from the estate when the loan is repaid after the Grant of Probate has been issued.

In cases where no tax is payable and a Grant of Probate is issued, the Capital Taxes Office has 35 days in which to request a full account. The Capital Taxes Office do make random checks. If a Grant of Probate is issued and no request is received from the Capital Taxes Office within 35 days of the date of issue then the estate is cleared of any obligation for Inheritance Tax. It is therefore best not to distribute any monetary legacies or sell any property, vehicles or valuable assets until at least 35 days after the Grant of Probate is received.

If tax is payable, then it is necessary to apply for a clearance certificate from the Inland Revenue.

Grant of Probate
The Grant of Probate will be sent to you together with the additional sealed copies you have requested. The Grant of Probate will be affixed to a copy of the will and will bear the embossed seal of the Family Division of the High Court of Justice.

Once a Grant of Probate has been issued, the Probate Office has no further responsibility in the matter and cannot help you with any enquiries regarding the estate.

14

AFTER PROBATE

Once you have obtained the Grant of Probate or Letters of Administration and the estate has been cleared for tax purposes you can begin to make applications for the monies and assets available to be released to the estate.

Bank Loan
If there has been a bank loan to cover the payment of Inheritance Tax this will be attracting daily interest and should be paid as soon as there is sufficient money in the account. The bank should be advised as soon as Probate has been obtained.

Estate Bank Account
An executor's bank account can be opened. This is usually given the name of the executor and the name of the deceased such as 'Mary Green Executrix of Jenny Smith deceased'. The bank will require to see a sealed copy of the Grant of Probate, the Will or Letters of Administration and evidence that the executors are the persons entitled to deal with the estate. It will also require personal references in the normal course of its business. A current account can be opened and the bank will issue a paying in book and a cheque book.

It will take some time to accumulate all the monies due to the estate, particularly if there is property and vehicles involved. It might be advisable to open a deposit account as well as a current account so that interest can be obtained. The bank can advise on this.

All monies received and any money held, such as cash found at the home of the deceased, money received from the sale of household possessions and lottery ticket claims, can then be placed into the current account before final distribution.

If the deceased had a bank account you may wish to use the same bank, but a new account in the name of the executors of the estate will have to be opened and any monies held in the name of the deceased can be transferred from the old account to the new executors' account.

Keeping an Account

A written account must be kept by the executors of all monies received and all amounts paid out. This should be given to all the beneficiaries when the estate has been settled. An example of a simple account is shown in Fig. 6. The account can be accompanied by photocopies of all financial transactions but if these are numerous they could be offered to those beneficiaries who wish to see them with the originals being made available for inspection. If there is property to be sold it could take quite a time for the final accounts to be available.

The executors will have to pay outstanding debts out of the monies received before distributing the legacies. Official receipts should be obtained for all monies paid out. In some cases if the will was made many years earlier, the financial situation of the deceased may have changed and it may not be possible to pay out all the legacies. This will be shown when the accounts are finalised and the beneficiaries can see a copy of the will and the accounts. In this

Received	£
Sale of House less Mortgage Repaid	66,000.00
Insurance Policies	1,500.00
Sale of Car	850.00
Cash at Bank (Current Account)	550.50
National Savings Deposit Account	23,750.00
Income Bonds	5,000.00
Sale of Household Goods	350.00
Premium Bonds	1,500.00
Sale of Equity Shareholdings	5,496.58
Pension	625.00
	105,622.08

Paid Out		
Funeral Expenses	2,570.20	
Telephone	41.30	
Credit Cards	280.50	
Garage Rent	80.25	
Gas and Electricity	70.55	
Probate Fees	140.00	
Executor's Expenses	580.15	
Monetary Legacies in Accordance with Will	10,500.00	
	14,262.95	(14,262.95)
Residue of Estate		£91,359.13

Fig. 6. Simple Executor's Account.

circumstance, all debts, including the legacies are paid out of the residue of the estate. If the residue is exhausted, then debts have to be paid from the pecuniary legacies, which are proportionately reduced. If these are all used up and debts remain, then specific legacies are reduced proportionately too. A solicitor's advice is definitely needed.

When applying for payment of bank accounts, insurance policies or anything else that is due to the estate of the deceased, the executors should request that cheques be made out to themselves as executors of the estate of the deceased so that they can be paid into the new account.

Shares

Once Probate is obtained, the shares can be transferred to the appropriate beneficiary named in the will (perhaps the surviving spouse) or sold by the estate and the proceeds distributed appropriately. For the former, first write to the Registrars to the Company (named on the share certificate or dividend counterfoil), requesting a stock transfer form. If the shares are worth less than £2,000 and the estate is valued at less than the Probate threshold (Appendix III) ask for a small estates form as well. Send back the form(s) appropriately filled in and signed, together with a sealed copy of the Grant of Probate (which will be returned to you) and the share certificate(s). Make sure your instructions are clear and the name and address details of the beneficiary are complete. Keep photocopies of everything you send and use recorded or special delivery. Then if documents signed for at the other end are lost, it becomes their responsibility.

Shares can only be sold through a stockbroker or share dealing service. You can find them in the business pages of the telephone directory or you may already know of one or have received personal recommendation for a particular firm. Reputation is very important as not all such firms carry the same level of client indemnity cover.

Make sure you understand how much commission may be deducted from the proceeds, whether there are any other contract or registration fees as well or whether a flat, all-inclusive fee is all that will be charged. It is best to compare such costs between several firms before going ahead.

Saga Share Direct (Appendix II), for example, will deal with the sale of shares for a fixed, one-off fee, based on the amount for which the shares are sold. You can phone them for a helpful information package which will come with the necessary transfer forms and details of their service.

The process for selling shares is the same whichever stockbroker or service you choose and most such firms will be efficient and helpful, especially if you are unfamiliar with the routine. Basically, you need to send the share certificate(s), together with a sealed copy of the Grant of Probate and a completed share transfer form to the stockbroker or share dealing service, and request that the shares be sold and a cheque in settlement in favour of the estate sent on completion of the deal.

Most banks have a department that will assist with the sale of shares. If you are in any doubt, you could seek the assistance of a solicitor.

Insurance Policies

Claims for payment of insurance policies can be made by sending the policies, and payment books if there are any, together with a sealed copy of the Grant of Probate to the companies concerned.

Banks

The sealed Grant of Probate should be taken or sent to the relevant banks. Request that all accounts be closed and the money either paid directly into the executors' new bank account by direct transfer from bank to bank, or a cheque sent for the executors' account. If the accounts to be closed were deposit accounts, interest will be included in the amount to be paid to the executors.

Building Societies

The sealed Grant of Probate together with payment books or statements should be taken or sent to the building societies with a request for the accounts to be closed and a cheque sent in favour of the executors' account.

Premium Bonds

Premium bonds can be retained for one year from the date of death, but must then be cashed; they cannot be transferred into another name. A sealed copy of the Grant of Probate, together with the premium bonds or confirmation of the ownership of the bonds which you may have obtained from the Premium Bonds Office (see the Appendix II) should be sent to the Premium Bonds Office with a request for repayment.

National Savings

A sealed copy of the Grant of Probate together with the account books, bonds and certificates should be sent to the National Savings Office (see Appendix II). Free pre-paid envelopes for this purpose can be obtained from post offices. The National Savings Office should be asked to close the accounts and send a remittance for the monies due with interest calculated to the date of death.

Funeral Account

If it has not already been paid and no arrangement was made with a bank to pay this directly from the account of the deceased, the invoice of the Funeral Directors should be paid as soon as there is sufficient money available in the account.

Credit and Store Cards

If there are any amounts owing against credit and store cards, these will now have to be repaid from the estate.

Jewellery and Valuable Items

Should it be necessary, jewellery and valuable items can now be sold. If there are members of the family who might like to acquire certain pieces, they could be offered at a price agreed by a professional valuer.

Vehicles
If any vehicles have been bequeathed by the deceased they can now be handed over together with the vehicle registration documents. Those documents, together with a sealed copy of the Grant of Probate, can then be sent to the licensing authority to request a transfer of ownership. If the vehicles form part of the residue of the estate, they may have to be sold and can be placed on the market for sale.

Headstone or Memorial
Arrangements can now be made to pay for any headstone or memorial that has been requested. Payment should not be made until the memorial has been inspected and the inscription is correct.

Final Distribution
When all the monies have been gathered into the executors' account and all the outstanding debts have been discharged, the final distribution of the monetary bequests according to the will can take place.

Before making a final distribution, make sure that all the debts have been paid and all the bequests dealt with.

APPENDIX I

DEATH OUTSIDE THE UK

When someone dies abroad (possibly from a sudden illness or an accident) and you are with them, you should contact the police immediately and also the nearest British Embassy or Consulate. If you are on holiday and staying in a hotel, inform the hotel manager and ask him to send for a doctor and to contact your holiday representative.

It would be helpful if you could engage the services of an interpreter if you have only a minimal knowledge of the local language. Being able to order meals, to make yourself generally understood in a language and to get the gist when someone speaks slowly, does not equip you to cope with legal and statutory matters.

You will be asked to produce the deceased's passport, travel documents and insurance documents. Keep them all together and make sure that they are returned to you every time you show them. If they are taken by the police or local authorities, ask for a receipt and for the name of the person to whom they are given.

Normally, people on holiday have holiday insurance and printed information will be found on the policy giving advice on what to do in the event of death abroad. There may be an international telephone number or main help-line number in the United Kingdom which you can contact for assistance. If the deceased, or you yourself, have a credit card, there may be a helpline telephone number which you can contact. Do not be distracted by the foreign language and surroundings. Listen carefully to what you are told and try to follow the instructions.

Far Eastern countries and some European countries have differing statutory and religious requirements and these will have to be observed. In some countries it may be a requirement that the deceased can only be identified by the next of kin. If this is required, the British Consulate will advise you. They will request the name and address of the next of kin and arrange for them to be notified.

In any event, you should get in touch with the family of the deceased to let them know what has happened as soon as possible. If you think you will have to stay abroad longer than you intended, contact your friends or family at home and let them know what has happened. The holiday representative will be able to make the necessary arrangements for your extended stay and can also organise your eventual return home. If you are travelling without the assistance of a holiday representative, you will need to make your own hotel and travel arrangements. These matters will entail certain costs but they should all be covered by your holiday insurance.

Once the British Consulate has been notified, they will give you all the advice and assistance you need. The Consulate can advance a small sum of money in an emergency but are not able to pay for any costs. They are not able to assume responsibility for payment of any sums of money that may be payable to doctors, ambulances, or other statutory bodies. They will, however, arrange a loan if you can prove that you have sufficient money at home to cover that loan. You will probably be requested to sign an acknowledgement that any sum loaned will be repaid.

When all the local regulations have been complied with

and a doctor's certificate of death (or the local equivalent) obtained, the death can be registered locally and also at the Consulate or Embassy. If registered at the Embassy or Consulate, the death will be entered in the Register of Foreign Deaths. A death certificate similar to that issued by the Registrar in England will be issued in due course and will be available at the General Register Office in England. The Consul will be able to give you all the necessary details. If the death is not registered at the local Consulate or Embassy, there will be no record in the United Kingdom of that death. The only evidence will be the death certificate issued by the local authorities. This may be in a foreign language and a certified translation will be required for a burial or cremation to take place in the United Kingdom, or any claims to be made there. It is therefore essential to register the death at the British Consulate or Embassy.

Arrangements can be made to transport the deceased home as soon as it is practical. This is a time consuming and expensive process, but it should also be covered by the insurance policy. Most insurance companies will be able to advise on this.

If repatriation of the body is not covered by insurance and there is insufficient money to cover the cost, the alternative, which would be less costly, would be to arrange for cremation in the country of death. The ashes could then be taken back to the United Kingdom. However, cremation is not available in all countries.

Death at Sea
If a death occurs on a ship, the death will be recorded in the ship's log. If the ship is a foreign-registered ship, death is considered to have taken place in the country where the ship is registered and is classified as a death abroad. The nearest British Consul should be contacted when the ship

docks. The ship's captain will have advised the harbour
authorities before arrival.

If the death occurs in a British-registered ship the death
will be recorded in the ship's log. Information will be given
to the Registry of Shipping when the ship arrives at its next
port anywhere in the world. The death will be reported to
the local coroner who will then advise what actions are
necessary.

Death in the Air
If a death occurs on a plane, it is considered to have taken
place in the jurisdiction of the country to which the aircraft
belongs. If the plane is not diverted elsewhere, the matter
will have to be dealt with when the plane reaches its
destination. The captain will radio ahead so that you will
be met and advised what to do on arrival. Usually arrangements will be made for a representative of the airline to
meet and assist you. If abroad, the British Consul will meet
and advise you. If the landing is in the United Kingdom,
the local police and coroner's officer will take over.

APPENDIX II

USEFUL NAMES AND ADDRESSES

Funeral Ombudsman Scheme
26/28 Bedford Row
London
WC1R 4HE
Tel: 020 7430 1112
www.funeralombudsman.org.
  uk
email: fos@dircon.co.uk

National Association of
  Funeral Directors
618 Warwick Road
Solihull, West Midlands
B91 1AA
Tel: 0121 711 1343
www.nafd.org.uk
email: info@nafd.org.uk

Funeral Standards Council
30 North Road
Cardiff
South Glamorgan
CF10 3DY
Tel: 029 2038 2046

Society of Allied and
  Independent Funeral
  Directors
SAIF Business Centre
3 Bullfields, Sawbridgeworth
Hertfordshire CM21 9DB
Tel: 01279 726777

Cruse Bereavement Care
Cruse House
126 Sheen Road
Richmond
Surrey TW9 1UR
Tel: 020 8940 4818

The Samaritans
See local phone book.

Compassionate Friends
53 North Street
Bristol, BS3 1EN
Tel: 0117 953 9639
(helpline for bereaved parents)

National Association of
  Bereavement Services
2nd Floor, 4 Pinchin Street
London E1 1SA
Tel: 020 7709 9090

INQUEST
Ground Floor
Alexandra National House
330 Seven Sisters Road
London N4 2PJ
Tel: 020 8802 7430

HM Inspector of Anatomy
Room 614
Department of Health
Wellington House
Waterloo Road
London SE1 8UG
Tel: 020 7972 4551
Fax: 020 7972 4791

British Organ Donor Society
BODY
Balsham
Cambridge
CB1 6DL
Tel: 01223 893636
www.argonet.co.uk/body

National Association of
  Memorial Masons
27a Albert Street
Rugby
Warwickshire
CV21 2SG
Tel: 01788 542264

Asian Funeral Service
209 Kenton Road
Harrow
Middlesex HA3 0HD
Tel: 020 8909 3737

Natural Death Centre
20 Heber Road
London
NW2 6AA
Tel: 020 8208 2853
www.naturaldeath.org.uk

Quakers
Friends House
173/177 Euston Road
London NW1 2BJ
Tel: 020 7663 1000

National Savings
Bonds and Stock Office
Blackpool FY3 9YP
Tel: 01253 793414
For Premium Bonds

National Savings Bank
Boydstone Road
Glasgow G58 1SB
Tel: 0141 636 2053

National Savings
Savings Certificates & SAYE
  Office
Milburngate House
Durham DH99 1NS
Tel: 0191 386 4900

National Association of Bank
  Customers
PO Box 15
Caldicott, Newport
NP26 5YD
Tel: 01292 430009

Saga Share Direct
The Saga Building
Middleburg Square
Folkestone
Kent CT20 1AZ
Tel: 0800 214 834

FT Information Services
Tel: 020 7825 8000
To obtain the Stock
  Exchange Daily
  Official List

Probate Department
Principal Registry of the
  Family Division
First Avenue House
42-49 High Holborn
London WC1V 6NP
Tel: 020 7947 6983
(answerphone for ordering
  Probate forms)
www.courtservice.gov.uk

The Capital Taxes Office
Inland Revenue
Ferrers House
PO Box 38
Castle Meadow Road
Nottingham NG2 1BB
Tel: 0115 974 2400

HM Land Registry
Lincolns Inn Fields
London
WC2A 3PH
Tel: 020 7917 8888

The Passport Office
Clive House
70 Petty France
London SW1H 9HD
Tel: 0870 241 1902

Driver & Vehicle Licensing
  Agency
Swansea
SA6 7JL
Tel: 0870 2400 009

Society of Genealogists
14 Charterhouse Buildings
Goswell Road
London EC1M 7BA
Tel: 020 7251 8799

APPENDIX III

INHERITANCE TAX AND PROBATE FIGURES

The following figures were correct at the time of publication; however, they are periodically increased for inflation and other purposes so please check the latest figures with the appropriate authorities.

If the estate does not exceed £5,000 it is not necessary to apply for Probate.

The standard Probate fee is £130. There is no fee if the estate is less than £5,000.

The threshold at which Inheritance Tax becomes payable is £234,000.

INDEX